Bible woodcut, Jost Amman, Frankfurt, 1587
Collection of Charles and Elizabeth Prothro

THE HEROIC PARADOX

THE HEROIC PARADOX

Essays on Homer, Sophocles,
and Aristophanes

By

CEDRIC H. WHITMAN

*Edited
and with an Introduction by
Charles Segal*

Cornell University Press

ITHACA AND LONDON

First published 1982 by Cornell University Press.
Published in the United Kingdom by Cornell University Press, Ltd.,
Ely House, 37 Dover Street, London W1X 4HQ.

International Standard Book Number 0–8014–1453–9
Library of Congress Catalog Card Number 82-5155

Printed in the United States of America

*Librarians: Library of Congress cataloging information
appears on the last page of the book.*

*The paper in this book is acid-free, and meets the guidelines
for permanence and durability of the Committee on Production
Guidelines for Book Longevity of the Council on Library Resources.*

Contents

To express over and over again the advent of Being,
permanent and in its permanence waiting for man,
is the only matter for thought.

—MARTIN HEIDEGGER, "Letter on Humanism"

Preface

Over the last ten years of his life, a life cut short by sudden illness in June 1979, Cedric Whitman lectured frequently to university audiences. The essays in this volume, with one exception, are edited from the texts of these talks. They expound and develop the conception of heroic humanism that he explored in his four books on Greek literature. Only the second piece has been previously published, and that not in a very accessible place. Anne Whitman conceived the idea of publication and entrusted the papers to my care. Without her concern, devotion to her husband's memory, and thorough familiarity with his work this volume would not have been possible.

Five of the essays arose as lectures for general audiences—hence the occasional informality, witticism, and personal anecdote. This lighter style, however, does not at all detract from their seriousness as interpretations of some of the major texts in Western literature. Indeed, the informal tone adds to their charm and will recall to those who knew Cedric Whitman the quiet humor, controlled intensity, and brilliant insights of his conversation.

Essays 1, 3, and 6 were in nearly final form and needed only minor stylistic revision, the location of references and quotations, and the occasional modification of the kind of remark that lecturers allow themselves in oral presentations but would recast

for publication. The fourth and fifth pieces required more extensive editorial work. In the essay on the *Antigone* I was able to
draw on an earlier version, which Marsh McCall of Stanford
University generously made available to me. It was necessary to
remove a few inconsistencies that Whitman, had he been able
to give the manuscript his *summa manus*, would have attended
to himself. Essay 4, which is valuable, I believe, as a clear, brief
statement of Whitman's latest views on the Homeric Question,
was originally much longer and contained considerable overlap
with Essay 3 and with his book on Homer. I have pruned what
seemed to duplicate material published elsewhere and kept what
seemed most useful to have in this concise form. The second
essay, "Existentialism and the Classic Hero," the only one previously published, appeared in *Das Altertum und jedes neue
Gute: Festschrift für Wolfgang Schadewaldt zum 15. März
1970*, ed. Konrad Gaiser (Stuttgart, 1970), pp. 99–115. It is
reprinted here (with minor changes) with the kind permission of
the publisher, W. Kohlhammer Verlag, Stuttgart, West Germany.
I also thank Harvard University Press for permission to quote
several long passages from Whitman's *Sophocles, Aristophanes
and the Comic Hero*, and *Euripides and the Full Circle of Myth*
on pages 12–13 in my Introduction.

Aside from the excisions and changes mentioned above and
minor stylistic changes, I have left Cedric Whitman's words as
he wrote and spoke them. Those who knew him will perhaps
take some pleasure in being reminded of his conversational
style. Whitman intended footnotes only for Essays 4 and 5, and
I have followed his indications (mostly brief and sometimes
cryptic penciled notes in the margin of the typescript) as closely
as possible. Here and there I have added supplementary material or included an obvious reference; these additions are en-
closed in brackets in the footnotes. Obviously much fuller
documentation was possible but seemed out of keeping with the
nature of the volume. An editor cannot take the place of the
author, and no doubt there is much that Whitman himself

would have improved had he lived. Even so, the results are by no means unworthy of the memory of a superb Hellenist and a sensitive literary critic of classical Greek poetry.

I owe thanks to my colleagues at Brown University, Michael Putnam and William Wyatt, for helpful suggestions and for additional reminiscences of Cedric Whitman. I am grateful to the editorial staff of Cornell University Press for their interest in these essays. I particularly thank Allison Dodge for incisive and sensitive copy-editing. The Press's anonymous reader offered useful suggestions. Linda Aro of Brown University did valiant service in the preparation of the manuscript. My greatest debt is to Anne Whitman, whose cheerfulness and courage in the face of adversity and undimmed love of learning are an example and an inspiration. Her own "heroic spirit" lightened the sad *pietas* of this task.

CHARLES SEGAL

Providence, Rhode Island

Abbreviations

Diehl: Ernst Diehl, ed., *Anthologia lyrica Graeca* (Leipzig, 1925), 2 vols.

DK: Hermann Diels and Walter Kranz, eds., *Die Fragmente der Vorsokratiker*, 6th ed. (Berlin, 1952), 3 vols.

Page: Denys Page, ed., *Poetae melici Graeci* (Oxford, 1962).

West: M. L. West, ed., *Iambi et elegi Graeci* (Oxford, 1971–72), 2 vols.

Other Greek authors are generally cited or translated from the Oxford Classical Texts where such are available.

Introduction
by Charles Segal

Cedric Whitman lived very much in the culture of his own time. He returns repeatedly to the theme of alienation, never inappropriately or clamorously, but with a steady concern for the problem of living an authentic life at times of social disintegration and widespread individual malaise. His belief in man, as his books make clear, comprehends the knowledge of human suffering, fragility, and despair alongside the knowledge of the inner strength that overcomes them.

Greatness of soul and the towering individual's relation to his own humanity and to society are leitmotivs in all of Whitman's work, from *Sophocles: A Study of Heroic Humanism*, published in 1951, to *Euripides and the Full Circle of Myth*, a collection of essays published in 1974. Though he was not blind to the destructive side of the heroic (for Whitman carefully studied its tragic dimension), his last two books stress the imaginative vision of a new kind of order, more personal and more tentative, in a confusing and chaotic world. Over the years his work moved from the bright glare of epic and tragic heroism in Homer and Sophocles to the more fragmented and kaleidoscopic world images of late Euripides and Aristophanes. This movement corresponds perhaps to his own increasing sense, in the later years, of life's absurdities. But even in these sometimes darker moods his conviction of the fundamentally moral significance of literature stands firm, and his love of beauty in art, his remarkable feeling for language and literary form, and his wonderful sparkle of humor shine through.

Like all of Whitman's criticism, these essays touch profound issues, the meaning of life and death, decision and commitment, the loneliness and the exuberance of living intensely and holding fast to one's truest self. They also show a rich appreciation of laughter and fun. The last essay in the volume, with its playfully ambiguous title, is perhaps the clearest testimony to Whitman's own resilience of spirit and warm humor, his delight in play, and his ability to elicit from Aristophanes' text its poetry and its earthy vitality. It also shows his ability to say penetrating and important things with an almost conversational ease, arresting and at the same time natural.

The notion of the hero that pervades Whitman's work is the center of one of the most powerful clusters of ideas that Greek culture has bequeathed to Western literature and art. It is also a principal target of a major movement in contemporary criticism which seeks to replace the person with the discourse of the person and to deconstruct the individual into mental categories, strategies of representation, and linguistic forms.[1] In such a perspective Whitman's ideas will no doubt seem old-fashioned. Yet if his emphasis on the individualism of the Greeks is at odds with current trends, it is no less useful as an interpretive tool for understanding the *Iliad*, Sophoclean tragedy, and Aristophanes' comedies. Amid all of the valuable new insights brought by the more sociologically and linguistically oriented criticism of the

1. See, for example, Michel Foucault, *The Order of Things: An Archaeology of the Human Sciences* (New York, 1973), Foreword to the English ed., xiii–xiv; Frederic Jameson, "Imaginary and Symbolic in Lacan: Marxism, Psychoanalytic Criticism, and the Problem of the Subject," *Yale French Studies* 55/56 (1977):338–95, esp. 381–83. For a recent example see Vincent Farenga, "The Paradigmatic Tyrant: Greek Tyranny and the Ideology of the Proper," *Helios* 8, no. 1 (1981):1–31. One thinks also of the fragmentation or dispersion of character in the *nouveau roman*.

past decade, the problem of the hero and the heroic character remains a key issue.[2] Even if some scholars would now phrase Whitman's questions differently and use different terms, his study of the hero's place at the limits of human society and normal discourse continues to be indispensable and exciting.

In Whitman's view, the hero, unprotected by religious orthodoxy or dogmatic faith, confronts the ultimate questions of life in the largest terms, experiences the deepest sense of self in isolation and suffering, and refuses to constrict the greatness of his nature and ideals to suit convention and so-called normality. "No Greek ever became a god, and no true Greek ever gave up trying" (*Aristophanes and the Comic Hero*, p. 58). In its tragic form that insistence on the autonomy of will and ideal rejects all compromise and chooses death or suffering over submission or conformity. Homer's Achilles and Sophocles' Ajax, Antigone, and Philoctetes are the purest examples. What Whitman calls the metaphysical dimension of the hero is his closeness to the gods, in a mysterious intermingling of favor and hostility. This heroism is itself "a divine force that gives [the hero] his dignity and supremacy and compels his death" (*Sophocles*, p. 79). Or, in the case of Achilles, the very intensity of the drive toward full self-realization "achieves the form and authority of immanent divinity, with its inviolable, lonely singleness, half repellent because of its almost inhuman austerity, but irresistible in its passion and perfected selfhood" (*Homer and the Heroic Tradition*, p. 182).

The gods are a part of the hero, a kind of inner divinity. Their special relation to the hero appears in the association between Zeus and Achilles in the *Iliad* (*Homer*, pp. 225ff.), in Athena's

2. For recent discussions see Patricia Easterling, "Character in Sophocles," *Greece & Rome*, 2d ser., 24 (1977):121–29; John Gould, "Dramatic Character and Human Intelligibility in Greek Tragedy," *Proceedings of the Cambridge Philological Society* 204, n.s. 24 (1978):43–67; Charles Segal, *Tragedy and Civilization: An Interpretation of Sophocles*, Martin Classical Lectures 26 (Cambridge, Mass., 1981), pp. 8–9.

closeness to Odysseus in the *Odyssey*, and in Heracles' to Philoctetes in Sophocles' play of the same name (*Sophocles*, pp. 187–
88, 190). At the same time the gods are also symbols, for want of
a better word, of a mysterious remote truth, "predicates of
experience—deified images of the way things are" (*Euripides*,
p. 81). In Homer they embody the untempered brightness of
existence itself, the relentless facts of being, the very condition
of mortal life in this world. They are at once the foil to the harsh
necessities of mortality and the stern enforcers of these necessities. In Sophocles the gods reflect the mystery against which
the hero collides in his search for absolutes. In Euripides they
are as elusive and many-faceted as the shifting meanings of the
world itself. In the tragic outlook of Homer and Sophocles they
frame the hero's sufferings in the dimension of eternity; they
also bear witness to his integrity and to the largeness and truth of
his choice and action. By their very removal from mortal decision and its consequences they define the essential qualities of
suffering humanity.

Even from these brief remarks it is clear that Whitman's
conception of the hero is far from a one-sided idealization of the
great or the lonely individual. He sees the hero in the context of
a wide range of complex theological and philosophical issues.
These issues are the concerns of the essays in this volume, as of
his earlier books, and they give his work a richness and depth
that no summary can satisfactorily render.

It was a brilliant leap of imagination to apply this conception
of the hero to Aristophanic comedy. There the aspiration toward inward divinity through man's own spiritual force, determination, and devotion to an ideal is transferred to the creative
fantasy of the poet and his hero. As in tragedy and epic, the
"comic hero" finds himself in a life-denying, chaotic, and
instinct-destroying world. He triumphs by holding to the im-
pulses of authentic selfhood, which in Aristophanic comedy
coincide with common-sense desires for peace and plenty. In
this triumph he achieves his wholeness as a human being and

remakes the world in accordance with his own vision of the meaning of existence.

In its comic mode, this exercise of heroic freedom includes a healthy portion of roguery or *ponēria*. *Ponēria* is, of course, totally at odds with the heroic ideal of an Achilles, an Ajax, or a Philoctetes. What the comic hero shares with his tragic counterpart is not the means but the end: the largeness of his aims, the commitment to a vision of the self and the world that challenges the existing condition of things, a limitless energy in pursuing his quest to free life from the confusion and clutter of the inessential, and the determination that ultimately can transfigure the world. Strange as it may seem, comedy exhibits, albeit in different terms, "no less of a triumph over external and apparent reality than does the revealing exultation which follows upon the tragic hero's moment of final knowledge" (*Aristophanes*, p. 279).

Whitman's greatest overall contribution perhaps lay in opening classical studies to new critical ideas, methods, and vocabulary. *Homer and the Heroic Tradition* made it possible for American classicists to approach formula and simile with a new sensitivity to imagery, symbolism, and formal design. It set a direction for a whole generation of Homeric studies that still has not been exhausted. *Aristophanes and the Comic Hero* realized the inconceivable, a systematic contemporary literary criticism of Old Comedy. Obviously there were predecessors and comtemporaries, and Whitman was not entirely a voice crying in the desert (in Sophoclean studies, for example, one thinks obviously of the books of Goheen, Kirkwood, and Knox published in the fifties). But the depth, elegance, and wealth of detail with which he studied the authors gave his work a definitiveness and an authority unattainable by more narrowly focused studies or individual articles. To have published three ground-breaking and monumental books in less than fifteen years is an achievement not easily repeated.

Few classicists in the fifties or even the early sixties were
reading Heidegger, Susanne Langer, or Northrop Frye, to say
nothing of applying them to the ancient texts. In both *Homer*·
and *Aristophanes* Whitman drew on the New Criticism's study
of image patterns, but escaped its dangers of mechanical
cataloguing or limited focus on the smaller units of expression.
He infused into the method his brilliant intuitions about poetic
imagination and drew on his own fine sense of intellectual
history, in part through the influence of Werner Jaeger and
John H. Finley, Jr.

Homer was the first major work in English to extend the
implications of oral narrative to a systematic criticism of the
Iliad and to articulate and practice an oral poetics of Homer.
Whitman performs that task brilliantly in his discussion of the
"snowballing" effect of the Homeric formula, the significance
of repeated similes, like that of the "dark-watered spring" at the
beginning of Books 9 and 16, and the symbolic implications of
elements like fire and water. His elucidation of underlying patterns of action and meaning beneath the surface detail has
paved the way for recent studies of the *Iliad* and *Odyssey* by
scholars like Michael Nagler and Norman Austin.[3]

Aristophanes was no less innovative. Before it appeared there
were a few scattered literary studies in English, but nothing that
integrated the fantasy, imagery, symbolism, and structure of the
comedies into a total vision on such a scale. The notion of
comic heroism enabled Whitman to restore to Aristophanes his
deserved place among the poetic geniuses of Western literature.
By stressing the creative fantasy and expansive transformation of
reality in the plays, Whitman brought to Aristophanic studies a
new appreciation of the imaginative brilliance of these works,
their "boundless artifice," their wonderful zaniness, and the

3. Michael N. Nagler, *Spontaneity and Tradition: A Study in the Oral Art
of Homer* (Berkeley and Los Angeles, 1974); Norman Austin, *Archery at the
Dark of the Moon: Poetic Problems in Homer's Odyssey* (Berkeley and Los
Angeles, 1975).

forgotten beauty of their poetry. The last essay in this volume shows Whitman's continuing gusto for Aristophanes and his ability to convey new facets of that poet's unique mixture of earthiness and airy fantasy. By pointing out the similarities between the roguish trickery of the Aristophanic hero and the Karaghiozes figure of the nineteenth-century Greek shadow plays (which Whitman studied in some detail), he also reminds us of some neglected continuities between ancient and modern Greece.

If in the perspective of thirty years *Sophocles* seems less revolutionary, that is only because its results have been so fully absorbed into the mainstream of critical thinking about Greek tragedy. By jettisoning the deeply rooted idea of the tragic flaw in his celebrated chapter on *hamartia*, Whitman opened the way for appreciating what is genuinely tragic in the Sophoclean hero and for laying appropriate stress on the irreducible core of irrational suffering. The whole conception of the hero, with its shifting and interlocking relations of weakness and strength, isolation and inner divinity, commitment to the ideally human, and self-destructive passion, enlarged the horizons of Sophoclean scholarship in ways that are still being explored. The opening chapter of *Sophocles*, a magisterial survey of earlier views of Sophocles and a general consideration of his religion and the nature of Sophoclean "humanism," has been translated into German in a major anthology of Sophoclean scholarship; the last chapter, on the *Oedipus at Colonus*, has also been anthologized in a collection of major essays on the poet (see the Bibliography).

The first two essays in this volume clearly develop from the conception of the hero elaborated in *Sophocles*, particularly its existentialist strands. In the tragic world of Greek drama meaning is not a given, but is created by man and within man from the stuff of his own life and his suffering, from the triumph of will over suffering—what Whitman called, à propos of the *Electra*, "the soul's use of time" (*Sophocles*, p. 150).

As some reviewers objected, Whitman occasionally takes too
optimistic a view of the hero and his triumphant vindication by
divinity.[4] On the *Trachiniae*, for example, he tends to place the
locus of heroism in the gentle Deianeira rather than explore the
harsh and problematical heroism of Heracles. But the achievement easily outweighs the faults. Every chapter has its share of
valuable details, challenging interpretations, and subtle reading
of action and character, for example, the opening chapters on
the "classic" and *hamartia* and the closing chapters on *aretē*
(the ideal of excellence) and humanism. The implications of his
remarks on the meaning of Sophocles' abandonment of the
Aeschylean trilogic form and on the creation of "a new kind of
evil—the evil of an unbearable self for which one is not responsible" (p. 143), extend far beyond Sophocles.

It is too early to assess the influence of *Euripides and the Full
Circle of Myth*, published in 1974. It is less ambitious than its
predecessors, and its study of the three "romances," *Iphigenia
in Tauris*, *Ion*, and *Helen*, is perhaps distinguished more by
sensitive observations of detail than by a radical new departure
in critical method. But Whitman always has something new
and important to add to previous interpretation. In *Euripides*,
he offers fresh views of Euripides' variations on mythic themes
and a valuable corrective to the Nietzschean image of Euripides
as a destroyer of tragedy. The concluding chapter, "The Scope
of Myth," is an extraordinary tour de force in its broad yet
well-digested survey of attitudes to myth and the mythic hero
from Aeschylus through Euripides. Although Whitman emphasizes the diversity and fragmentation of the heroic personality in the Euripidean corpus, he also demonstrates that there is a
positive side and an intensity both religious and poetic in
Euripides' questioning of the traditional gods and in his ex-
perimentation with new types of plot (see pp. 120–21). As he

4. For example, G. M. Kirkwood, *Phoenix* 7 (1953):41; see also Gilbert
Norwood, *American Journal of Philology* 74 (1953):172–73 (both reviews of
Whitman's *Sophocles*).

remarks of the three romances near the end of the work, Euripides was possibly "surprised to find himself rediscovering myth as a pattern of some kind of whole, arising out of the wisplike tatters of a world strewn across a steadily receding sky" (p. 136).

These general remarks hardly do justice to the wealth of individual observations and insights that make Whitman's work of abiding value to all students of Greek literature. For all his brilliant elucidation of imagery and symbolism, some of his shrewdest insights are on character. One thinks of his studies of the conflict of mother and daughter in the *Electra* (*Sophocles*, pp. 158–59), of Agamemnon, Achilles, Ajax, and the minor characters like Idomeneus and Diomedes in the *Iliad* (*Homer*, chs. 8 and 9). Then there are his incisive one-liners: "Every Homeric *aristeia* is a character-sketch" (*Homer*, p. 158); Menelaus is "the most cared-for man in the army" (*Homer*, p. 232). I should mention also his scrutiny of Dicaeopolis, Socrates, and Philocleon, among others, in *Aristophanes*; his remarks on the spiritual reintegration within Helen at the departure of the cloud-Helen (*Euripides*, pp. 42ff., 63ff.); the portrait of mother and son in the *Ion* (*Euripides*, pp. 79ff.); the rapid but forceful sketch of the hero of the *Hippolytus* ("the bright splinters of Hippolytus' self-admiring mirror," *Euripides*, p. 119).

Never shirking the critic's final task of estimating literary value, Whitman is not afraid of making judgments, always based on wide and careful reading in both modern and ancient literature. Not everyone will agree that the "*Andromache* is perhaps the least elevated work that has come down to us" (*Euripides*, p. 123), or that the characters of Euripides' so-called patriotic plays are "paper thin" (ibid., p. 131), or that the *Clouds*, in its present form, is essentially an artistic failure (*Aristophanes*, pp. 123ff., 143). Yet such judgments, though controversial, are challenging.

Combining a poet's feeling for language with a scholar's acumen, Whitman has a flair for the brilliant *mot juste*, for example, his superb description of the Homeric simile as "rising like a prismatic inverted pyramid upon its one point of contact with the action" (*Homer*, p. 103) or his comparison of the combination of epic formulae to "the falling of glass chips in a kaleidoscope" (ibid., p. 124). Readers of his *Aristophanes* will savor the account of the poet's speech in Plato's *Symposium*, "a myth mingled of Empedocles, impertinence, and hiccups, yet embodying a wistfully hilarious image of human desire" (p. 15). In a more somber vein is the description of Homeric fate "which casts a mysterious light of inevitability upon all that happens" (*Homer*, p. 228) or Homer's gods as "a kind of imagery" which "lends to all humanity a fourth dimension, not of time, but of eternity, the essence of the heroic vision of glory and permanent value" (*Homer*, p. 238).

I resist the temptation to multiply examples, for the present volume has its share of such moments. Whitman has the gift of compressing years of reading and thought into a single iridescent crystal of perceptive utterance. More remarkable still is his combination of this level of stylistic brilliance and intuition with a full grasp of philological and historical issues. *Homer* is probably his most impressive achievement in integrating the poetic and scholarly sides of his nature. The first five chapters, fully a third of the book, are a masterly survey of the Homeric Question in all of its linguistic, archaeological, and historical complexity. That and his other books, especially *Sophocles* and *Aristophanes*, locate their respective playwrights in the intellectual, political, and social crosscurrents of their time. The chapter "Sophocles and the Fifth Century" and the discussions of the relationships of the *Birds* and the *Frogs* to their intellectual milieus (*Sophocles*, pp. 221–40; *Aristophanes*, pp. 173ff., 253ff.) show the apparently effortless grace with which Whitman integrates complicated material into the clarity of a large vision that is both imaginatively perceptive and historically accurate.

In his writing, as in his life, Whitman carried his learning easily. He treated knowledge not as a massive block of erudition with which to crush an opponent, but as something warm and vital, supple with life and energy. Even his technical articles and reviews, listed in the Bibliography, show the same deft balance between philological detail and humane significance. He assimilated his wide reading into an active command of literature that seemed to come spontaneously as needed, whether he was citing the Babylonian Creation Epic, the Persian Book of Kings, Thomas Mann, or Gertrude Stein. He could adduce, with equal appropriateness, Edward Lear's "The Pobble Who Has No Toes" and Mozart's *Don Giovanni* (*Aristophanes*, pp. 171, 231). Humor enlivens all his books, as it did his talk. He can unobtrusively slip in a delightful witticism about *Ion* as a "foundling father" (*Euripides*, p. 105) or lighten an argument with a sparkling anecdote. His superb knowledge of music and his particular love of Mozart are apparent in the many musical parallels he draws throughout his work.

For all his familiarity with the great literary classics, he can find the right place for Buster Keaton and Charlie Chaplin. He is unaffected enough to indulge a personal fondness for Laurel and Hardy and custard-pie slapstick in the midst of a discussion of Salvador Dali and surrealism (*Aristophanes*, p. 275). Whitman was keenly aware that Aristophanes in his own time was popular entertainment, albeit of a very special sort, and that in our time he should yield at least a little fun.

Whitman's gifts as a translator should not go unmentioned. His scholarly books contain long passages of skillful verse translation. In one sense they are a form of criticism parallel to the rest of his exposition. His rendering of the prologue of the Taurian *Iphigenia* is an integral part of his point about its "tremulously emotional tone" (*Euripides*, p. 3):

I thought in sleep that, parted from this land,
I dwelt in Argos, and among my maids
Lay sleeping, but the back of earth rolled quaking,
And I arose and fled outside and saw
The palace copestone falling, and the whole roof
Stricken in ruins from pillar tops to floor.
One only column in my dream was left
Of the ancestral hall, and from its cap
Let down gold locks, and took a human voice,
And I, honoring this rite I have of slaying
Strangers, sprinkled him as one death-devoted,
Weeping.

His splendid version of the opening lines of the *Trachiniae*
perfectly catches the tone of solemn foreboding that Deianeira's
speech sets for the entire play (*Sophocles*, p. 107):

There is an ancient saying among men,
How none can know this mortal life, if it
Be good or evil, till it ends in death;
But I, though not yet come to Hades, know
My life is heavy and ill-starred.

His translation of the parode of the *Birds* conveys the note of
wistful remoteness and delicate unreality in the play's pastoral
music (*Aristophanes*, p. 178):

Consort mine, come rise from sleep,
Scatter strains of holy song
From divine lips, wailing Itys
Yours and mine, for whom we weep.
As your quivering throat is shaken
By your sacred melodies,
Purely through the leafy bindweed
Goes the echo to Zeus' dwelling,
Where the golden-haired Apollo,
Listening, answers your lamenting,

Plucks his ivory lyre, and stations
Dances of the gods, and onward
Through the immortal mouths, harmonious
Flows the singing of the Blest.

Fortunately, thanks to Anne Whitman and Michael Putnam,
his sensitive verse translations of a number of *Odes* of Horace
are now published in a limited edition (see Bibliography).[5] Several of the essays in this volume contain new verse translations,
some extensive, which Whitman, as was his custom, made for
this purpose.

Whitman's brilliance of imagination and expression at times
occasioned resentment or hostility. Classical scholars are sometimes resistant to new approaches and retain a literalist bias, an
unfortunate holdover from the positivism and scientism that
sparked the necessary and important philological, historical,
and textual achievements of the nineteenth and early twentieth
centuries. Precisely because he challenged received ideas so powerfully and with so scintillating a style, he was singled out as an
especially dangerous representative of risky, unsound new ideas.
But from the first his books assumed and held a position of
leadership in the field, and public recognition came quickly: the
American Philological Association Award of Merit for *Sophocles*, the Christian Gauss Prize for *Homer and the Heroic Tradition*, two Guggenheim fellowships, appointment to the American Academy of Arts and Sciences and to the Academy of
Literary Studies, and numerous other honors.

Of the six essays in this volume the title piece is the key to the
unity of the collection. It brings together, in synoptic form,

5. In addition to the long extracts translated in his critical writings, Whitman also made complete verse translations of Euripides' *Alcestis* and *Ion*
(unpublished), the *Pervigilium Veneris* (only one copy printed), and several of
the longer Homeric hymns. It is hoped that these may eventually be published.

Whitman's conception of the hero and covers the three authors he studied in depth. The figure of the hero allows him to define the changing relations between individual and society and the tension between human needs and the will of the gods in the latter half of the fifth century. He traces the heroic ideal from the self-assertive absolutism of the *Iliad* to the moral conflicts that form the substance of tragedy.

The second essay focuses more narrowly on the hero of tragedy. Moving from Nietzsche's criticism of the moralistic and rationalistic view of tragedy to existential philosophy, especially Heidegger's, Whitman locates the tragic heroism of the fifth century B.C. in the dark currents of a nonrational demand for absolutes. But what transmutes that heroism into the most powerful dramatic poetry of Western literature is a "vision of timeless being," expressed through the still vital symbols of myth and, quoting Heidegger, "the spirit of sacrifice [which] takes upon itself kinship with the imperishable." This essay also extends Whitman's view of tragic heroism to Aeschylus, with valuable comments on the *Seven against Thebes*, *Prometheus Bound*, and *Oresteia*.

In the third essay, written in a more leisurely style, we turn from tragedy to epic and from character to plot construction. Whitman tackles the major problem of oral poetics, how the bard composing within the traditional, highly formulaic poetry of early epic verse achieves the coherence and artistry of a work like the *Iliad*. He resumes some of his points about image clusters and associative patterns from the central chapters of *Homer and the Heroic Tradition* and goes on to show how Homer modulates from one episode to another, conflates traditional stories and themes, and draws upon his audience's knowledge of traditional materials. There is a cogent parallel with the technique of the Yugoslav oral tradition and a brilliant point about the foreshadowing of Achilles' death when he slays Hector by driving his spear through a vulnerable place in the armor that is in fact his own. The fourth piece, in a rather more technical vein, answers some of the Analysts' attacks on the unity of the *Iliad*, in which Whitman firmly believed ("Credo in unum Homerum," he once wrote with a playful glance toward F. A. Wolf, "factorem Iliadis et Odysseae, credibilium omnium et incredibilium"). This essay also sets forth his latest thoughts on the controversial question of how a more or less authentic text of an orally composing Homer has come down to us in its final form.

Essay 5 returns to tragedy and the themes of the first two essays with a detailed scrutiny of the *Antigone*. Exploring the heroine's complex relation to nature (*physis*), Whitman examines the play's definition of man, placed between Promethean mastery and subjection to the unknown forces of both the gods and himself. Sophocles is here exploring the tragic necessity of man's defeat by nature and yet his triumph over nature, a triumph won not through the technology praised in the Ode on Man but through the power of soul.

In Whitman's view the so-called double burial, one of the notorious interpretive problems of the play, is a single act with a double agency, both human and divine, that reflects the unique and mysterious bending together of God and man that lies at the heart of Whitman's conception of tragic heroism. Antigone acts in willful defiance of one kind of order, but at another level moves in sympathy with the divine laws of a nature that reverberates with the meaning of her choice and her suffering.

The concluding essay, in a lighter vein, shows Whitman's brilliance and wit as an interpreter of Old Comedy. In one of his finest insights he restores Aristophanes to his place as a poet of the city in a series of city poets that includes Juvenal, Ben Jonson, Baudelaire, and Joyce. This is a poetry at once ethereal and concrete, distilling the essence of fifth-century Athens and also speaking the voice of the alienated individual who emerges there with the strains of the Peloponnesian War, the voice "of the individual heart at bay."

In his imaginative re-creation of the world this type of hero can bring forth his triumph even from the rags and tatters of Euripides' isolated outcasts. Unlike the satiric figures of Ben Jonson, who laid bare the iniquities of an unregenerate society, the Aristophanic hero is a little and ordinary man who resiliently musters humanity, joy, and common sense against the Goliath-like complexity of urban alienation. Though focusing mainly on *Acharnians*, *Birds*, and *Lysistrata*, this essay gives an overview encompassing all of Aristophanic comedy. With its insight into dramatic structure, its appreciation of form and language, its illuminating modern parallels, and its flashes of wit and humor, it is Whitman at his most stimulating and most delightful.

Cedric Whitman exercised almost as great an influence through his teaching as through his publications. His teaching career spanned some thirty-three years, all at Harvard, where he moved from the rank of instructor to the Eliot professorship of Greek literature, which he held at his death at the age of sixty-two. During this period, one in which Harvard was preeminent in the study of Greek literature, a significant proportion of future teachers and scholars of classical Greek (the present writer included) passed under his tutelage. I remember the electrifying effect of his lectures on the *Iliad* in Greek 112, two years before the publication of his Homer book, when he was obviously carrying it all in his head. The clarity and the unpedantic assurance with which he integrated the archaeological, historical, and linguistic background of the Homeric poems seemed to me and my classmates little short of miraculous. The brilliant exposition of oral poetics (which then had no such exalted name), the accounts of the nature of the formula and the simile, the characterization of the figures of the *Iliad* and *Odyssey*, and the analysis of the structure of the two epics were a revelation. A few years later, as a graduate student, I experienced something similar in his seminar on Aristophanes. Twenty years ago it was still a novelty for a classicist to approach Aristophanic comedy as a literary text rather than a historical source book. Whitman made Aristophanes come alive as poetry and as genuinely funny comedy.

Although the essays collected here convey somewhat more of Whitman's personal side than his other books, what cannot appear from the printed page is the man's generosity, modesty, and unpretentiousness, the openness to new ideas, and the willingness to listen patiently and give his time and wise counsel to the most hesitant of his students. He had the rare capacity to be profoundly serious without taking himself too seriously. There was not a pedantic breath in his body. It is characteristic of his modesty that he regarded himself as "a classical humanist, not a professional expert on the Classics."[6]

Paradoxically this man who devoted his scholarly work to studying the austere reaches of the heroic personality was among the most approachable, unassuming, and instinctively kind of human beings. His slightly reserved, even shy manner made the warmth of his friendship all the more valued by those who came to know him well. Whitman directed numerous dissertations in Greek literature, some still in progress at his death. For most of his students his friendship, advice, and encouragement continued long after they left Harvard.

Despite the troubles of ill health in his later years, he and Anne maintained their Cambridge home as a place of good talk and warm humor amid the busy life of Harvard. Whitman became a bit more detached, a shade more ironical, but one could never be sure when some quietly meditated flash of wit would dissolve what a friend affectionately called his basset-hound solemnity into irresistible smiles and laughter. His conversation remained an endless source of broad culture, wise judgment of books and of people, and delightful, ironical, but

6. Whitman in a letter cited by John H. Finley, Jr., at the service in honor of Cedric Whitman, held at Memorial Church, Harvard University, Oct. 25, 1979, p. 5.

never cruel humor. His love of all things Greek, which extended from the *Iliad* to the Modern Greek Shadow Theater and contemporary Greek literature, shines forth in all his work, from the Sophocles book to his foreword to Terzakis's *Homage to the Tragic Muse*, published the year before his death.[7] In his written work, as in his teaching and his conversation, he conveyed an integrity of responsive scholarship and an informed sympathy that lift the reader or hearer to his own high level. His learning and literary sensitivity were so integral a part of him that he did not have to parade them. To make Homer, Sophocles, Aristophanes, and Euripides "relevant" (a word he detested), he had no need to make brash claims: they became relevant at once by virtue of the meaning he elicited from the texts.

What Whitman wrote of Euripides in the last of his books to be published in his lifetime may also be said of Whitman himself: "The spirit conquers through the transmutation of experience... into knowledge" (*Euripides*, p. 140). Of his own conquests of the spirit, achieved by the transmutation of facts into knowledge, the present volume is a rich, if inadequate, memorial.

7. Cedric H. Whitman, Foreword to Angelos Terzakis, *Homage to the Tragic Muse* (Boston, 1978).

1. The Heroic Paradox

The title of this essay is an attempt to put into a phrase what seems to be one of the most fundamental aspects of Greek civilization, or at least of that earlier part of Greek civilization, which extends from Homer's time to the end of the fifth century B.C.: namely, the idea, and the problem, of the heroic individual. After the fifth century, the steady and thorough development of systematic, philosophic thought had the effect of resolving all paradoxes by reason; our paradox today, however, is not a philosophic one, but one that belongs to those unsystematic but vigorous founding fathers of Greek thinking, the poets. Later on, the elements of poetic thinking were analytically separated off as concepts and categorized, so that certain associative psychological complexes, which had been so compelling, lost their essential cultural force. But the earlier centuries of Greek culture were dominated to a great degree by the vision of the heroic; and by vision I mean precisely a psychological complex of aspirations, associations, and personal standards that, however contradictory they might be, were felt simultaneously as a single spiritual drive.

Perhaps this drive, or vision, in great part prevented the Greeks, though they were the inventors of political theory, from contriving any such durable political system as the Romans bequeathed. For the heroic tends toward the "anarchic," and

the hero feels himself to be a law unto himself; so that it follows
of necessity that the heroic and the idea of society are not always
at one—indeed far from it. As we shall see, the heroic attitude
reveals itself in a variety of relationships to society, as the latter
developed in Greece, from the eighth to the fifth century. And
it is these relationships, among other things, that I wish especially to trace and demonstrate here.

It is well, as Aristotle would say, to begin with definitions.
What is heroism? How do we define this complex of drives,
which I have referred to as a paradox? We do not mean simply
the megalomaniac hero who can swim for eight days and eight
nights over the Baltic Sea in full armor slaying whales all the
way—and such is Beowulf—for though such a character is undoubtedly admirable, the Greek heroic notion involves far more
than mere exaggerated physical prowess. It involves somehow
the totality of the human individual, writ large, of course, but
still representative of humanity in its individual consciousness.
As such, it becomes relevant to us. The hero is ourself, expanded for our inspection and understanding by the genius of
Homer and other poets and pushed to logical—or illogical—
extremes. And, as the Greek tradition presents him to us, we
see him motivated by two simultaneous, opposite needs: the
need for absolute status, and the need for human context,
commitment; or, as the Greeks would put it, the urge toward
divinity, and the necessity of remaining mortal. This is, one
might say, the essence of the paradox, and we shall try to illus-
trate its meaning and its results.

In *The Greek Experience* Sir Maurice Bowra draws a distinction between the heroic and the moral.[1] For we must admit, to
begin with, that the heroic will not always quite square with the
moral as we see it. Morality, as we have learned it from the
Decalogue and elsewhere, is a restrictive kind of code of behavior, one that says "Thou shalt not" rather than "Thou

1. Sir Cecil Maurice Bowra, *The Greek Experience* (London, 1957), ch. 2,
"The Heroic Outlook," esp. pp. 22–23.

shalt." (I am not offering any value judgments on this subject at the moment.) On the contrary, the heroic code, as we see it in its earliest form in Homer, says "Thou shalt," rather than "Thou shalt not";[2] it demands fulfillment rather than restraint of the self, yet not fulfillment of libidinous psychic "drives," but fulfillment of the self as a large thing capable of transcendent status, through *action* and adherence to *inner standards*. Thus though it does indeed differ from our moral mode, heroism is not simply the opposite of the moral, but rather a different kind of approach toward behavior, and toward the notion of what a person is. I hope to be able to draw together these two ideas, the heroic and the moral, and show that they are not necessarily and always mutually exclusive, but that they start in different ways, and may even, under some circumstances, coincide.

But first, to return to the motivation of the heroic: we mentioned as one element the urge toward divinity, a kind of wish to be a god or to be godlike. In the twentieth century, given our ironical mode of standing apart and regarding ourselves as odd varieties of Freudian aberrations, this may not seem very practical. We do not think of ourselves as possible gods. But the Homeric princes apparently did. And there was therefore in their psychology a theory of the self, the self as transcendent, the self as somehow divinized, somehow equaling the gods. And this idea is reflected very strongly in the Homeric epithets θεείκελος, "godlike," θεοειδής, "looking like a god," or just

2. [Bowra, ibid., p. 22, observes that the demands of the heroic outlook often have the force of "the most rigorous categorical imperatives" and sometimes do not "differ from those of ordinary moral codes"; but, he goes on, "honour and morality differ on important points of principle," especially in that "honour is more positive than negative; its obligations are more to the fore than its prohibitions." For other views of the conflicts and contradictions between morality and honor, society and individual, inherent in the heroic ideal of early Greek culture see E. R. Dodds, *The Greeks and the Irrational*, Sather Classical Lectures 25 (Berkeley and Los Angeles, 1951), chs. 1 and 2; A. W. H. Adkins, *Merit and Responsibility: A Study in Greek Values* (Oxford, 1960); Alvin Gouldner, *Enter Plato: Classical Greece and the Origins of Social Theory* (New York, 1965).]

simply θεῖος or δῖος, "divine," epithets constantly applied
to the heroes in Homer. On the other hand, there is also a
passionate knowledge, a desperate self-knowledge, among all
these heroes, that they are mortal and that they are destined to
die. So, on the one hand, they feel the need to be like the gods,
and on the other hand, they know perfectly well that they must
fulfill their mortality. And this was even more of a paradox and
a difficulty for the early Greeks, who had no doctrine of the
immortality of the soul, than it is for us, because for the Greeks
the difference between gods and men is not specifically good-
ness or wisdom: it is not that the Greek gods are better than we
are morally, nor is it that they are more wise, or even always
more powerful. (Some of the gods get wounded on the
battlefield by the better heroes in Homer.) The specific thing
that distinguishes the gods is *immortality*. This is the absolute,
intransigent fact, from which there is no escape. The gods are
immortal, and men are mortal. Nonetheless, however per-
versely, the hero feels like an immortal, and the epithets traditionally used by the bards to mean either "divine" or "like the
gods," imply a kind of absolute status which the hero strives to
gain.

This is one of the most besetting problems imaginable, and it
stands right at the beginning of Greek culture. W. K. C.
Guthrie in his excellent book *The Greeks and Their Gods* said
that there was one central problem. He devoted a whole chapter
to it, albeit only a four-page chapter.[3] The central problem is
precisely this: Did the Greeks think that to aspire to be like the
gods was a hopeless piece of dangerous presumption, or did they
feel that it was a necessary and inevitable spiritual urge? Guthrie
very sensibly does not try to answer this question because it is
unanswerable. Certainly the Greeks never answered it. It is,
however, an extremely important question to raise, for it illus-

3. W. K. C. Guthrie, *The Greeks and their Gods* (London, 1950), pp.
113–16.

trates the unresolved inconsistency of the Greeks in this matter. The Greeks constantly thought of themselves as striving for the immortal, striving for absolute status, while on the other hand, we meet with very frequent admonitions against trying to be a god. One of the most famous of ancient Greek maxims was γνῶθι σεαυτόν, "Know thyself." What did this mean? We must not interpret this in modern terms, meaning "Be self-analytical" or "Examine your feelings and attitudes about life," though it began to mean that after Socrates had promulgated introspective thought. Originally all it meant was "Know that you are mortal and not a god"; "Know your limitations."

In Greek literature we find many paradigms of presumption and downfall. Pindar, for instance, tells the story of Bellerophon, who, after he had conquered the Chimera, tried to ride his winged horse up to heaven, whereupon Zeus struck him down with a thunderbolt. Herodotus constantly reiterates the same ethic. The motivation of King Xerxes, especially as outlined in Book 7, is extremely subtle, but Herodotus makes quite clear that those whom the gods wish to destroy they first make mad. Xerxes is the prime example of a mortal whose pride led him to godlike behavior, which led him to destruction. There are also the familiar maxims: "Do not try to climb the brazen heavens"; "Do not try to be Zeus in vain"; "Do not try to marry golden Aphrodite"—though, of course, every man would like to. And yet, though Bellerophon was destroyed for flying, one must fly; one must aspire. Pindar, from whom I just quoted most of these sayings, identifies himself in many a poem with a flying bird, and these images of flight reflect the feeling he had along with all other true Greeks, the need to transcend, the temptation of the brazen heavens. He who does not feel this is, as Pindar says, "earth-breathing." He is not living up to what is expected of the individual. For it is the individual who is the decisive force in these earlier centuries of Greek history. And it is because of this individualism that the hero is important. He is the paradigm, the myth of the individual—you, me, and everyman—in his feeling, as a friend once said to me, which everybody has, that he is at once the best and the worst, the highest and the lowest of all human beings. And it is this, precisely this kind of intuition of one's self that is framed in the *Iliad*.

I need not relate the story of the *Iliad*. I will first say, however, that when Achilles quarreled with Agamemnon it must not be thought that it was a matter of a first lieutenant being insubordinate to a general. The two stood in no such relation to each other. The leaders of the army before Troy were an assembly of princes, for the most part quite independent of each other. They were, in fact, peers. They were all individuals together, and it is important to remember that their social system depended upon the idea of mutual individual respect. It is true that their tokens of respect were somewhat materialistic. A hero's honor was concretely represented by the quantity of his booty—tripods, horses, pots and pans, gold, bronze, and women.

Now, what Agamemnon does in the first book of the *Iliad* is take away from Achilles a woman, a token of honor. We are told elsewhere in the poem that Achilles has other reasons for prizing this woman, indeed that he loves her, as other men love their wives, though she is only a captive. But the reasons are irrelevant here. What is relevant is the crucial moment in Book 1 when Achilles, enraged at Agamemnon's breach of the social structure, the mutual respect of warriors for each other's honor, begins to draw his sword on the king. Why does he not kill Agamemnon? Why does he put his sword back in its sheath? Certainly not because he hesitates to kill a king or fears any consequences. Throughout the *Iliad* Achilles gets away with everything. But Athena comes down and restrains him. As always in Homer, the appearance of a divinity broadens the mortal's vision, be it of power or of knowledge. Suddenly Achilles sees the whole matter in a wider range, from a universal perspective in which his very being has been called into ques-

tion. Now he must ask after the meaning of himself and of all
men, their honor and their aspirations, in the light of final and
absolute divine standards.

Athena betokens the divine standard, and Achilles pursues it
by his appeal to Zeus. It is like a question, almost a challenge to
the great god, to define in ultimate terms the heroic aim. Achilles asks: What is honor, what is heroism, what is a man? His
challenge is to prove his absolute indispensability by his absence
from the war; let the Greeks be defeated and learn. At this point,
Achilles enters the heroic paradox. He asks for divine sanction
upon individual heroism and upon his honor, but at the same
time he dismisses his whole commitment to the Greek host,
almost to humanity itself. Here is the individual asserting himself against society, in a way that threatens to make him no
longer relevant to it. As Nestor says later, "Achilles alone will
derive benefit from his valor" (*Iliad* 11. 762f.). A man may assert
his divine absolutism and thus in some sense "become a god,"
but then also after some fashion he ceases to be a human being,
and he has no communication with anyone.

Achilles lives out the paradox that way so perfectly put by
Guthrie in his book: divinity and mortality are irreconcilable,
but for the Greeks they are inseparable. (I don't suppose any
Greek ever really became a god, but I know some who don't give
up trying even today.) And this form of heroism, which is
paradoxical in statement, becomes dilemma in action. The
hero's problem is to act out his heroism. The heroic aspiration
to godhead was common to all the heroes of the *Iliad*, but
Achilles was the only hero who lived out its underlying assumption. The demand on the hero is very rigid: "How shall I by
action, in myself in all its mortality, somehow vindicate my
intuition of likeness to divinity?" This is the most extreme form
of heroism, and the *Iliad* is the only poem, so far as I know, that
portrays heroism in its full tragic effect. The demand of heroism
sounds like confusion, but it is not. It is a fine, perilous
balance—a paradox, demanding action and terminating in

self-abnegation, not to say self-destruction. The other heroes may compromise a little, but Achilles is rigid because the heroic demand is rigid in its insistence on the necessity of an absolutism on the one hand and human communication on the other.

When discussing the heroic paradox, I'm reminded of an episode in James Thurber's book *The White Deer*. Prince Jorn, the third son, rides off desperately wanting to have a terrible dragon to slay, or a terrible ice mountain to climb and a princess to win, or a terribly difficult riddle to solve. And he comes to a stone Sphinx sitting on a pillar. He says, "Ask me a riddle." The Sphinx, of course, deals professionally in riddles, and says, "All right. What's whirly, what's curly, what's pearly early?" So Jorn answers without any hesitation, "Gigs are whirly, cues are curly, and the dew is pearly early," and he rides on. Then he turns back and says, "What was hard about that?" and the Sphinx says, "It was hard to say it without moving my jaws." Well, this, in a way, is a paradigm of the true intellectual situation: it is not the question that is difficult; it is the rigidity of the questioner, the rigidity of the underlying idea, and this is what Achilles faces. Achilles is himself the rigid questioner.

The problem does not become immediately acute. Achilles is content and well satisfied, no doubt, by the defeat sustained by the Greeks in his absence. His divinity, his cause sustained by Zeus, is showing itself. But in Book 16 his humanity comes to him in the form of Patroclus, invoking his pity for fellow human beings. Lordly as he is, Achilles is touched. He had sworn not to help the Greeks until the Trojans had come to his own tent and ships, but he is willing for Patroclus to give them a little respite. Thus Achilles can keep to the letter of his absolutism, while yielding to his humanity; he lends something of himself when he lends Patroclus the armor. But there is a sharp and agonizing division of his will at this point, as the irreconcilables make themselves felt. The very defeat he wanted, to prove his own splendid greatness, is taking place, but his humanity is hurt by it. And so he tries, by sending Patroclus, to be both god and human at the same time. But he cannot; something must give way, and with the death of Patroclus, his situation changes.

It is only after Patroclus's death that Achilles can fully identify himself with that terrible godlike quality he had asserted in his appeal to Zeus, and to which Zeus had agreed. After Patroclus's death he can become, as he does, a terrible, murderous demon, driving the Trojans like locusts before a forest fire. Here is the absolute warrior, fulfilling literally the prayer uttered by several other heroes: "Would that I might slay as Zeus, Athena, and Apollo slay." Here is the godlike at its highest pitch.

But Achilles is doing something else too, something that contains the secret of his ultimate triumph, that makes his achievement more than a military exploit. What is important in the whole terrible death march that Achilles makes from Book 19 to Book 22 is that he knows he is destroying himself. He is sacrificing himself to the idea of himself, to the idea of his own heroism, as represented both in himself and in Patroclus. He is sacrificing himself, together with his victims, with a sense of total horror. He tells Lycaon, one of the younger sons of Priam, whom he had formerly captured, but ransomed and given back to his family, that now he is no longer interested in ransoming anybody, "because," he says, "I shall die too. Patroclus is dead; I shall die too some morning, some evening, when Zeus wills. But, my dear friend, die thou also," Ἀλλά, φίλος, θάνε καὶ σύ (21. 106). This is not savage bloodthirstiness. It is a kind of terrible knowledge of the universality of death. And what Achilles achieves for his absolute is the knowledge, and, more, the assertion of his own death.

It is universally felt that in Book 24, in the indescribably beautiful meeting with Priam, Achilles returns within the scheme of humanity once more, and indeed he does. He has not, however, by any means renounced his position; his absolute supremacy is clear. By what means, then, if any, can the coexistence of divinity and mortality be achieved in the heroic soul? The answer surely lies in what was said above about Achilles' assertion of his own death. Death is perhaps the only absolute that exists for man, in the final analysis, all else being relative and subject to change and circumstance; and perhaps the assertion of this absolute, its very choice, in fact, is the only assertion by which mortality and divinity can coincide, in a brief moment of transcendent self-knowledge. There is a speech by Sarpedon in the twelfth book of the *Iliad*, which seems to point to this answer. Sarpedon says to his kinsman Glaucus:

Good fellow, if we by fleeing this fray and surviving
Always might then be ageless and immortal,
Neither would I myself battle among the champions
Nor would I urge you on to the glorifying war;
Since as it is, all told, fatalities of death stand over us
Thousand-fold, whom no man's power it is to escape or avoid,
Let us go then, either to offer glory to some man, or ourselves gain
    glory.

[322–28]

The whole paradox is here: Honor is in action and self-risk. It is precisely because we can die that the battle is meaningful. Death is the catalyst of the irreconcilables.

But if this is the answer of the *Iliad*, it must be recognized that such a solution does not fit every occasion or every era. The *Iliad* treats the individual in extreme isolation and in such a conflict with society as reduces him to a shadowy minuscule. Clearly if society was to exist, there had to be other ways of treating the individual, in all his aspiration and dangerous search for absolute selfhood. The individual may, if he is tenacious enough, satisfy his heroic quest by the choice and assertion of his own death. Society, in contrast to the heroic individual, seeks continuity; and in certain other monuments of Greek literature, we find attempts to see heroism in the light of possible "livability."

The earliest of these attempts is the *Odyssey*. Achilles in the

Iliad says, "Go to, I am honored by Zeus; therefore in some sense I am a god, and I will die of it." Odysseus says the opposite. Where we first meet him in Book 5 of the *Odyssey*, the nymph Calypso has kept him for seven years, a castaway doomed, for all we can tell, to everlasting obscurity. He enjoyed Calypso for a while, apparently, but now he is more than a little tired of her. Calypso offers to make him immortal and keep him with her forever. She says, "You know perfectly well that I am more beautiful than your wife," and Odysseus replies rather ungallantly, "Yes, I know, you are. I can't deny that." (It's probably better not to argue with these goddesses.) But he goes on to say, "Nevertheless, I want to go home; a man who is proper-minded wants to go home, and to recover his wife and his son" (5. 215–20). Now this is very humane and understandable. One might easily think at this point that Odysseus has no contact with the intransigent paradox of divine and human which confronted Achilles. Odysseus states his devotion to his family, to his human commitment, and that is a clear choice, unlike the self-dividedness of Achilles in Book 16 of the *Iliad.* But Odysseus has his conflicts too.

Throughout the poem, or the first half of it anyway, he is torn between the will to return to Ithaca and the curious desire for knowledge and experience which leads him into so many adventures with other peoples, with monsters, and with divinities. He must have these contacts with the "large world," as one might call it, but in the long run, they are instruments in making him the man most capable and effective in a "small world," namely, his home in Ithaca. These contacts with the deathless enlarge him, surely, but the idea of divinity does not swallow him up. And thus he solves the heroic paradox by choice, not by conflation—and perhaps for this reason he emerges in a more understandable light than does Achilles. Odysseus chooses the human, despite the obvious temptations of being immortalized and living for the rest of eternity in a lovely island with a beautiful goddess. And the island *is* lovely, as Homer describes it, full of rich trees and fresh fountains. But for a Greek it would be a hard place to live—no people on it, no ships to provide adventure; most of all, no politics. This would be the wrong kind of divine status. Odysseus needs and wants the human scene, and his temptations toward divinity are ultimately restricted by his feeling for the human estate, with all its struggle.

Odysseus does indeed have his own contact with death, in the eleventh book, when he is invited by Teiresias to foresee his own death. But his choice of death is a choice of death as the end, the natural end, of a life process he is living out and dignifying by all that he gives to it. By contrast, Achilles chooses his own death as a way to deny and abnegate a process that is, he feels, unworthy of a person who is like the gods. So in the *Odyssey*, we have a different kind of hero, one who points much more toward the historical period. Odysseus asserts moral and social values, though somewhat after his own fashion. He kills the suitors, who are bad fellows, reestablishes his wife and his family, and he dissolves the paradox of the divine and the human by choosing the human and rejecting the divine. This choice signals a whole new kind of hero in relation to society.

I mentioned Bowra's view that the heroic and the moral were distinct. Yet they are not always and necessarily totally opposed. We see in Odysseus the first step, one might say, toward the moralizing of the hero, the attempt to bring the idea of the great man within some kind of a social scheme whereby life may be seen as in itself satisfactory. And yet the triumph is not total. The *Odyssey* is a wonderful poem, but if it be asked, What is the society that Odysseus fits into at the end? the answer is hard. What is left? Odysseus has wiped out a considerable portion of his island's future leaders; and what he asserts in his victory is not a social contract, but rather the tremendous heroic return of a patriarchal monarchy. Society as such does not count for much. The *Odyssey* shows the effort of the Greek mind to get the idea of the great man somehow within a social structure where everybody can live; but there was more to be said than could be dramatized in the *Odyssey*. The old heroic monarchies did not return, and in the rising city-state of the seventh and sixth centuries B.C., the problem of heroic temperament continued to occupy the attention of the poets (who were the thinkers) of the times. In particular, there are Tyrtaeus, the poet laureate of Sparta in the seventh century, and Solon, the great poet-legislator of Athens in the sixth.

Tyrtaeus is a rather obscure fellow. Some people in antiquity said he could not have been a Spartan, that he must have been an Athenian. That is only because they thought that Sparta never could have bred a poet, but Tyrtaeus seems to me just the kind of poet that Sparta would have bred. Sometime around the turn of the seventh century the Lycurgan constitution went into effect and transformed the whole culture of Sparta into a military oligarchy of formidable, but arid, efficiency; Tyrtaeus seems to have been the poet of the new regime. It is interesting that he uses the language of Homer, the magniloquent epithets and so forth, but they serve now to exalt the picture of a "citizen-soldier" who is of no individual importance whatsoever, except insofar as he stands in his ranks and fights like his fellows. Somewhere, the great individual has gotten lost, though his use continues. Tyrtaeus saw the great man as someone who had to be suppressed, suppressed within the concept of the Spartan military phalanx. His idea of the great individual is the man who stands with his feet well apart, holding his shield before him and throwing his spear and biting his underlip with his teeth as a true Spartan should, or, if he loses his spear, hurling stones or anything else he can lay his hands on. A hero is a cog, at most a good cog, in a military wheel, not anything more. Especially fragment 9, if it is a fragment (John Finley once called it "the thirteenth chapter of First Spartans"), illustrates the feeling:

I would not say anything for a man nor take account of him
    for any speed of his feet or wrestling skill he might have,

Not if he had the size of a Cyclops and strength to go with it,
    not if he could outrun Boreas, the North Wind of Thrace,
Not if he were more handsome and gracefully formed than Tithonus,
    or had more riches than Midas had, or Kinyras too,
Not if he were more of a king than Tantalid Pelops,
    or had the power of speech and persuasion Adrastos had,
Not if he had all splendors—*except for a fighting spirit.*
                              [*Tyrtaeus,* 9 Diehl = 12 West]

"Though a man have the speed of foot of the wind, and the
strength of such and such, and the beauty of Tithonus and this
and that and the other thing," the poem says, "if he have not
ferocious battle valor, then I reckon him as nothing." Tyrtaeus
is attempting to reduce the individual, to bring his power within
the totality of the state. But something is lacking—the man
himself. If we look to the next century, we come to Solon of
Athens; and Athens, as always, is an infinitely more hopeful
place than Sparta. Solon, the great man who helped lay the
foundations of Athenian democracy (which was not so terribly
democratic, but was a tremendous step in that direction) saw the
individual as a kind of moral unit. He was suspicious of great
men, in the usual sense. "Through great men," he says, "the
city is destroyed, and the people have fallen under the hands of
a tyrant" (9. 3f. West). The tyrant, of course, was Peisistratus,
and the poem must have been written shortly after Peisistratus
had made himself tyrant. By great men, Solon means men of
irresponsibly boundless personal aspirations, including the unfortunate greed for wealth which seems to have characterized
the Athenian aristocracy.

    Solon was appointed in 594 B.C. to legislate between the
upper and lower classes in Attica, where a despearate economic
and political crisis had developed. He owed his appointment,
obviously, to the expectation of favor from both sides. As a man
famed for integrity, he could be expected to foster the cause of
the oppressed; as an aristocrat, he could be expected to favor the

aristocracy. Solon did neither. Instead, he reconceived the idea of the citizen, as a moral entity, equitably bound, whatever his estate, to universal, divine justice, and therewith to the welfare of the city and the welfare of himself. The details of his constitution need not detain us; what is important here is his conception of the heroically responsible citizen, the man of absolutism, but now in the service of society, instead of against it.

He himself provided the example. Since he refused to be partisan either to the aristocracy or the lower classes, he was attacked by both. In a beautiful poem preserved to us by Aristotle, he describes his effort, how he freed the divine earth of Attica from the boundary stones that represented the foreclosures of the rich upon the poor, how he brought back citizens who had been sold into slavery for debt and had been away so long they could scarcely speak Attic Greek any more (frag. 36 West). Then he says, "But I cast my protection over both parties, and stood at bay, like a wolf among dogs" (36. 26f.). In this poem, as in some others of Solon, one begins to hear foreshadowings of the issues of Attic tragedy, in particular of the moral heroes of Sophocles, sternly striving to assert, by their own vision and self-sacrificial stance, the basis of a viable society.

For a brief while at the beginning of the fifth century there is a sort of peace between the hero and society. The two are disparate from the start. The city is a corporate enterprise, a corporate engagement; the hero is an engagement between himself and the universe, and the two engagements do not always meet with ease, as they did in the mind, if not the experience, of the farsighted Solon.

The plays of Aeschylus are the work of a uniquely lofty, even visionary, mind. We cannot deal with them in any fullness here, but only observe one or two points relevant to his attitude toward Athens and the individual. Aeschylus, who had fought at Marathon, and probably also at Salamis, identified himself, body and soul, with the new, triumphant Athenian democracy and envisaged it as an order, divinely established, wherein justice for individual and society alike could be achieved.

The great, main scene in the *Eumenides* illustrates well how, for Aeschylus, the hero fulfills himself—not, as in Achilles' case, in direct terms with the universe, but through the institutions of the true political organization, conceived under the gods, and called Athens. Orestes, son of Agamemnon, having avenged his father's murder by killing his mother and her paramour Aegisthus, comes to Athens to be tried and acquitted of his crime. Though he has been ordered to this bloodshed by Apollo himself, it is significant that such direct divine sanction is not quite enough: Orestes must pass through some social, judicial process to obtain absolution, and even Apollo must appear in the role of a mere advocate. The individual may have his personal relation with a god, but such a relation finds completion only in the context of civic structure. Orestes is, in fact, acquitted; he is justified in his relation with Apollo; but it is through the city's agency, through a court especially instituted for the purpose, a corporate body found competent to adjudge and affirm heroic individual action and conscience, within a scheme of universal justice, presided over by Athena herself.

Aeschylus marks a rare moment in the history of Greek culture, a moment of painfully won harmony between the turbulent heroic spirit and the social need for order, stability, and coexistence. Aeschylus died in 456 B.C., and the generations that followed were of a very different nature.

When we come to the latter half of the fifth century, we meet the two younger tragic poets, Sophocles and Euripides, each with a different reaction to the whole idea of heroism. We can pass over Euripides because for the most part he has no use for heroes. Though one might find possible exceptions, it is fair to say that when Euripides is not reducing the heroic to ironical echoes, he ignores it altogether. But as the most articulate voice of the new age, he prompts us to ask after the nature of that age, to ask what had happened to the harmony we found in the previous years. What changed the whole situation? Why did not that fine balance of individual and society work? Why did not Aeschylus's vision of the individual hero within a social framework continued to avail?

All things change, of course, and as Thucydides says: πάντα γὰρ πέφυκεν καὶ ἐλασσοῦσθαι, "Everything has a natural tendency to decline" (2. 64. 3). But for one thing, the great intellectual revolution known as the sophistic movement changed a great many cultural attitudes in Athens. It was ·a highly intellectual movement, but its effects were not confined to intellectual circles. The actual theories that evolved can be reconstructed only with difficulty and careful research—and considerable disagreement—but the undeniable result of the sophistic movement was the end of archaic Greece and the beginning of that shift toward rationalism which developed into the philosophic age.

One of the first effects came from the Sophists' study of human nature, as a phenomenological object, so to speak, a study that entailed an immediate decline of religious, moral, and political values. The Sophists were studying nature, φύσις, which then meant primarily human nature, and they discovered that man was an animal. The suggestion is familiar to us, but it was a new discovery in the mid–fifth century. And it was rather a shock. Man was not only an animal: he was a dangerous animal, a totally immoral animal. Toward the end of the century, we find in the Sophist Antiphon a discussion of propositions that we may paraphrase as follows: "Of course you should obey the laws, as long as anybody's looking at you; but if nobody's looking at you, by all means follow your nature." "Fulfill yourself. Give yourself to yourself" (87 B 44A, col. 2 DK). We should carefully contrast these notions with Achilles' sacrificing himself to the idea of himself. The sophistic idea was quite different, implying, as it did, simple libidinous satisfaction; and by the influence of such individualistic and hedonistic views the bases of Athenian society were gravely enfeebled.

The first and the greatest of all the Sophists was Protagoras. He did not indeed say quite all these desperate things, but he led the way to them. What he did say was, "Man is the measure of all things" (80 B1 DK). Though nobody knows exactly what he meant by that, we all know the results of what people thought he meant by it. This anthropocentric view inevitably meant a shift in religious emphasis, if not total loss of religion.

Sophocles is very much a man of this period, and his whole treatment of the heroic is related to Protagoras's anthropocentric view. Sophocles is far from irreligious, but he is religious in a way that starts from the human soul. The development of the sophistic movement, with its attrition of all values, and the consequent decline of the dignity of the individual within society, forced some kind of spiritual revolution. If all society loses those luminous values that were so meaningful for Aeschylus, where does one look for order? What happens when the great Athenian state, which gave fulfilling scope to the heroic aspirations of the individual, the Athens that had fought off the Persians in 490 and 480, becomes an oppressive imperial city, a bureaucracy full of legal sharks, political entrepreneurs, and an increasingly less responsible, because exploited, proletariat? Whatever one may think of Pericles and his imperialistic policy, his ideal, articulated in the Funeral Speech that Thucydides attributes to him, balanced collective aims and individual fulfillment. The period after his death in 429 saw a rapid loss of that humane responsiveness so keenly admired by Aeschylus. And with that, what happened to the individual?

With the congealing of Athens' political and social institutions in the latter years of the Peloponnesian War, the individual began to be, in fact, alienated, to use our term. And in Sophocles' works there arises, as if to fill the gap, a new exploration of the inner life of the individual, and therewith a return of the heroic idea, a rebirth, one might say, together with all that is so paradoxical about the hero—his deep human commitment and his commitment to divinity. And it is significant that now, again, as in the *Iliad*, the hero is in conflict with society, no longer a part of it, but a pariah of sorts, who at once excels it and is trodden down by it. In at least six out of the seven extant tragedies of Sophocles, the individual stands heroically in conflict with the world with which he is confronted. Society no longer saves, as it did in Aeschylus. The individual must save himself, yet not as an entity for whom society has no relevance; rather as the embodiment of those values that, oddly enough, preserve society. That is, these heroes assert what is the basis of society. And this basis is a kind of new union of the idea of heroic self-assertion with what we would call morality. We began by drawing the distinction between heroism and morality. But in Sophocles the two somehow come together. In the midst of increasing chaos, to seek the source of order in the structure of the individual soul is to frame heroism in an image of moral selfhood, an image that combines moral, human, and social commitment, with large heroic self-assertiveness.

   The clearest example is still *Antigone:* Antigone is the holy lawbreaker, the saint. She is, as she says, ὅσια πανουργήσασα, the "holy transgressor" (74). She is protecting the bases of society by breaking its laws, in this case the morally indefensible edict of Creon. This edict represents the chaos that follows upon the idea of rule for rule's sake, the imperial principle of the stronger ruling the weaker. Many critics do not recognize the fact, but it is perfectly clear from the play that the gods come crashingly through on the side of the heroine; there is no trace of the ambiguity of values which has repeatedly been foisted on the *Antigone.* We have before us the image, the contemporary, historical image of the fifth-century individual, for whom political institutions are not only unresponsive but, indeed, tragically wrong. Creon is the image of the πόλις τύραννος, "imperial city," and I am sure that any subject islanders who belonged to the Athenian Empire at this point, who happened to see the *Antigone,* could not have failed to recognize Creon for what he is. And Antigone is the image of the citizen hopelessly impaled

upon the necessity of either moral integrity or total submission
to a system that lacked any justification in the bases upon which
society is supposed to be framed. This is what Antigone means
in her great speech about the eternal laws:

> For it was not Zeus who proclaimed this, nor
> Did Justice, dwelling with the gods below,
> Design such laws for men; nor did I think
> Your edicts ever might prevail so far,
> That one who is mortal could outrun the laws,
> Unwritten and unswerving, of the gods.
> Not just today or yesterday, these live
> Forever; no one knows from whence they came.
> It was not likely then that, out of fear
> Of any man's will, I should transgress these,
> Thereafter to be punished by the gods.
>
> [450–60]

Many people find Antigone an objectionable young woman,
just as many people find Achilles a mere egotist. But in point of
fact, both are moved into action by a perception of divinity in
the midst of a corrupted society, against which they rebel, in
favor of a social assumption under which an individual may find
honor and dignity. The great moral achievement of Sophocles
was that he could find an answer to his own times in a rededica-
tion of heroic selfhood to a universal ethic for humanity. If man
was to be the measure, let him, in Sophocles' own words,
"measure his course by the stars" (Oed. Tyr. 795). Divinity, so
to speak, is discovered in the greatness of human self-sacrifice,
even more clearly than it was in Achilles' willed self-
destruction. So Antigone in a sense divinizes herself by her
devotion to that which she feels to be basically humane. And it
is interesting that both Achilles and Antigone are somehow
summarized, by their respective creators, in the image of
Niobe, the bereaved mother, who turned into a weeping stone,
a thing no longer mortal, but full of mortal sorrow and compas-

sion (*Iliad* 24. 602ff., *Antig.* 823ff.). Death, sacrifice, and the
defiant eternal self are the tokens of the heroic, and without
them, no true Greek society could exist. Even in the unheroic
fourth century, Plato recreated the figure of Socrates in the
image of the earlier classical heroes.

It is this vision of moral salvation through self-sacrifice which
redeems society—at least, in the thought of Sophocles (it did
not happen historically). The final great example of this vision,
which I wish to mention briefly, is Oedipus. Oedipus, like
Antigone, finds his heroism in the context of a society that can
be saved only by a truly great man. The prologue to Sophocles'
first Oedipus play, *Oedipus Rex*, makes this explicit: the priest
appeals to Oedipus almost as to a god, to rescue his city from the
plague, as he had once rescued it from the Sphinx. But what
does Oedipus discover? He discovers that he is himself the un-
witting source of the whole trouble. Yet there is that driving and
absolute moral heroism in him which enables him to complete
his quest, despite all opposition, and to become, at cost of
everything to himself, the savior he promised to be. For in fact,
with the revelation of the murderer of Laius, Thebes is cleansed
of the plague, whatever happens to Oedipus. The hero may be a
parricide, guilty of incest, but the act of self-knowledge purifies.
Thebes is saved, and Oedipus, though ruined, is on his way to
an as yet undreamed salvation.

In the second play, *Oedipus at Colonus*, he begins from this
desperate pariahdom; having wandered for years, he comes to
Athens. Is the vision of Aeschylus returning to the ninety-year-
old Sophocles? Athens, indeed, saves Oedipus, and again, as
with Orestes, dignifies the man of moral suffering. But Oedipus
also saves Athens. His body, it is prophesied, will be a blessing
to any land in which it is buried, and he and Athens mutually
choose each other. This religious way of reintegrating the hero
is almost Aeschylean; but in Sophocles, there is a tremendous
emphasis on the importance of the individual, the hero himself,
who, blind and helpless as he is, possesses the godlike ability to

bless, or to curse, redeem, or destroy. The individual pariah has
at last become a god, for Oedipus was in fact worshiped as a
minor deity at Athens in the late fifth century and thereafter.
The heroic adherence to an absolute has actually divinized a
man, and made him a blessing to the city of his choice. Again,
the paradox cannot be solved without death, and Oedipus becomes a god only when he fulfills his mortality. But he behaves
like a god throughout the play, and his "death" is clearly a
"translation," not a "fall." The *Oedipus at Colonus* is perhaps
the greatest of all expressions of the heroic individual, with his
intuition of the divine, reshaping and revivifying the world. The
play is Sophocles' crowning reply to a contemporary society that
told the individual to go find his own way, if it bothered to say
even that.

The great and reassuring beauty of it all is that the humane
redeemer, who has measured all things, is nothing but a helpless old man, with no instrument except hard-earned, but true,
self-knowledge, and his own indomitable spirit. One is reminded of the remark in Marguerite Yourcenar's brilliant
Memoirs of Hadrian. The emperor says, "At this point I began
to feel that I was a god, because I knew that I was a man."[4] This
is a little like what Oedipus says: ὅτ᾽ οὐκέτ᾽ εἰμί, τηνικαῦτ᾽
ἆρ᾽ εἴμ᾽ ἀνήρ, "When I no longer exist, then indeed am I a
man?" (393). Man is somewhere between nothing and the gods,
and by the time Oedipus discovers that he is truly a man, he is
on the verge of becoming a deity. Indeed, the terms of Sophocles'
last work are scarcely any more those of society and individual,
but of humanity as a whole; the heroic paradox has become an
unfathomable religious mystery.

We have examined the heroic as it appears in tragedy and the
epic, but these somber forms were not the only ones in which it
found expression. The so-called Old Comedy, which flourished

4. Marguerite Yourcenar, *Memoirs of Hadrian* (1951), trans. Grace Frick
(New York, 1954).

in Athens through the fifth century, developed into a vehicle for many things, a unique medley of fantasy, lyric, satire, obscenity, and nonsense. And in the midst of all, there often appears a figure whom we may well call heroic, albeit comically heroic. I would like to mention two of these figures as examples of how Aristophanes responded to the cleft between the individual and the social and political structure in which he was situated.

The earliest extant play, the *Acharnians*, opens with the protagonist sitting all alone in the Pnyx, the place of public assembly, waiting for his fellow citizens to convene; the morning wears on and everyone is late. Meanwhile, the lonely individual—whose name, Dicaeopolis, means "man of public justice"—sits and recounts his sorrows, some of which are due to the war with Sparta and some to the wretched inadequacies of contemporary tragic poets. The isolation is itself significant, suggesting that the hero alone is the only responsible man in Athens, and so it turns out. When the people do convene, Dicaeopolis tries to introduce a proposal to make peace with Sparta, but he is rudely suppressed by the presiding officers, who have their own reasons for finding the war profitable.

There could scarcely be a more telling picture of the alienated individual, silenced and bound by the proliferating tentacles of corrupt statecraft. But the heroic spirit presently asserts itself. Abandoning the attempt to live within the political framework, Dicaeopolis manfully steps out of it, and makes his own private treaty with Sparta, for himself and his family. This liberating fantasy works so well that presently the hero is trading happily with the enemy and enjoying such contraband luxuries as roast thrush and Copaic eel, while the vain militarists stand guard in the freezing mountains and starve on garlic rations.

It may seem absurd to compare such a figure with the heroes of Sophocles, but they have at least this in common—that they tower over the society with which they conflict, and vindicate their right to differ with it. Dicaeopolis is sublimely successful and beats Athens to her knees. Aristotle says that the hero of comedy is a man of lower stature than ourselves; but as Dicaeopolis reels off the stage at the end, waving a flagon of wine and with a trollop on each arm, it is clear that he has achieved something like divine stature—though in very human terms.

Another example of alienation and reconciliation, just as heroically absurd, though now with a touch of real wistfulness, is in the *Birds* (414). Once more we meet a protagonist, Peithetaerus, who is alienated by the bureaucracy of Athens and decides to leave it for some better place. When no better place seems available, he and his companion decide to go live with the birds. This has a double significance in Greek, for on the one hand it is a return to nature, an assertion of the country with its innocence over the city with its corruption; and on the other, it is an acquiescence in those aspects of nature which for Antiphon, as we have seen, absolved man of all commitment to law and order.

The *Birds* is a superbly systematic construction of utter chaos, and the most beautiful of all Aristophanes' works. The story is a vicious circle: the two friends, who had abandoned Athens precisely because it had the drawbacks of an imperial city, proceed to build a bird-city in the air, designed to cut off the sacrificial smoke from the gods, and starve them into submission. As usual, Aristophanes replies to the world's absurdities with a transcendent, resounding superabsurdity. Here, Athenian imperialism has been transformed into an empire that subdues the gods themselves, and it is not long before the alienated, self-exiled Peithetaerus has grown wings and deposed Zeus; the play ends with his marriage to an allegorical lady whose name means "monarchy," and whose attributes suggest Athena. However one interprets the *Birds*—and it has been much disputed—one cannot fail to recognize the heroic quality of the myth and of the hero himself, the individual who asserts himself against society and in favor of his affinity for the divine. And if Peithetaerus's achievement is even more unconditional than that of his tragic brothers, Achilles and Oedipus, it is because a comic hero, being hardly more than the little man's Walter Mitty–like self-propulsion into grandeur, is bound by no rules or limits whatever, physical, political, and least of all, moral. In some ways, comic heroism is the purest, and most paradoxical of all.

One could continue at great length on the subject of the heroic, and the foregoing has been necessarily superficial. But the heroic idea, the vision of the transcendent individual self, went through many phases in the history of early Greece, until it all but vanished in the fourth century, to revive only at intervals in subsequent times.

The fourth century developed the sense of civilized, private life—"*il faut cultiver nos jardins*"—while politics, a field in which in the early fifth century every citizen had found a source of expression and self-fulfillment, became progressively the preserve of specialists. Expertise and philosophy are the keynotes of the fourth century, to such an extent that the Aristotelian concept of the πεπαιδευμένος ἀνήρ, "the cultivated gentleman," had to be developed as a counterbalance. But the whole spirit was different from the heroic times of the fifth and preceding centuries. Then, it was the individual, in all his paradoxical transcendence and weakness, who led, while the idea of society followed; and if society had too much the upper hand, rebellion was in order; sometimes the rebellion spelled little more than chaos, as with the "great men" whom Solon feared as irresponsibles. But it could also spell the reassertion of the bases of communal life, of the human idea, as with Antigone or Oedipus. But whichever way the process went, it illustrates the truth of what my friend the late James A. Notopoulos once said to me: "Every Greek is an anarchist."

2. Existentialism and the Classic Hero

It is not in itself surprising that certain contemporary French dramatists, notably Jean-Paul Sartre and others commonly called existentialists, have declared the affinity of their theater for that of the ancient Greeks, or that they have taken up the old myths for modern treatment, as in Sartre's *Les Mouches,* Giraudoux's *Electre,* and the *Antigone* and *Medea* of Anouilh. What is surprising is that they feel that the affinity lies in what, at most, is a doctrinaire mannerism not at all characteristic of the Greeks, namely, the rejection of character as a dramatic mode in favor of the skeletal formula of situation, choice, and denouement. In reality, these new French plays bear little resemblance to their models; and naturally so, for their mode is far from the heroic mode of antiquity, or, as Northrop Frye calls it, "the high mimetic mode." But between ancient tragedy and existentialism itself as a philosophy there exist some very clear affinities which, except for some remarks by Martin Heidegger, appear to have been rather neglected since Nietzsche; these affinities may be of some help in understanding certain Greek tragedies, especially those of Sophocles.

In *The Birth of Tragedy* Nietzsche wrote: "Consider the consequences of the Socratic maxims: 'Virtue is knowledge; all sins

I wish to express my thanks to Professor Hazel Barnes, who gave me helpful suggestions during the preparation of this essay.

arise from ignorance; only the virtuous are happy'—these three
basic formulations of optimism spell the death of tragedy."[1] In
subsequent pages, the philosopher expands in trenchant detail
upon the evils of interpreting tragedy from the point of view of
Socratic ethics, and his criticism pinpoints to a considerable
degree the sorry declarations of the last century about the meaning of Greek tragedy. Many people have felt that Nietzsche's
little book seems at times to be getting dangerously close to
rhetorical delirium, and that a more temperate statement might
have won more immediate respect for this aesthetic (and pes-
simistic) approach to the tragic question. But in the long run,
the critical wind has changed greatly; and scholars today,
though not so eloquent as Nietzsche, are becoming equally
willing to relieve tragedy of the frontal, foursquare moral re-
sponsibilities first imposed on it during the decades of its decline
in the fourth century B.C. The implication is not, of course, that
tragedy has nothing to contribute in the moral realm, but only
that in form and intention it tallies poorly not only with the
moral theory of Platonic and Aristotelian academism, but also
with its whole categorical system.

There is no need to rehearse here either Plato's objection to
the morals of tragedy or Aristotle's apparent effort to rescue
them. If there is to be such a thing as a philosophy of tragedy, its
premises must offer at least tolerable approximations of the motive and emotive forces of tragedy, its inherent states of mind as
expressed in the poet's symbols, and as comprehended in the
cultural milieu of its audience. Such states of mind, and their
attendant symbols, will of their nature be more equivocal, more
pliant, and more embracing than the moral categories as
analyzed by idealistic philosophy, and presented, according to
the determinants of mean and extreme, as ethical essences apart
and distinct from the agent or percipient. Since these states of

1. Friedrich Nietzsche, *The Birth of Tragedy* (1872), in Nietzsche, *The
Birth of Tragedy and The Genealogy of Morals*, trans. Francis Golffing (Garden City, N.Y., 1956), p. 88.

mind proceed from an era before the human personality had
been quite separated philosophically from its empirical involvement, the dynamic elements of Greek tragedy—character,
will, "fate"—can find adequate expression only in the synthetic
properties of symbol and myth. The latter modes treat people,
things, and events in their involvement with each other: they
grasp the character of Oedipus, for instance, as simultaneously
at one with his fate and at odds with it. From this point of view,
Greek tragedy, as a symbolic complex of action, will, chance,
environment, or whatever—in any case a complex representing
experience as totality—thrusts the challenging question of personal identity into an absolutely central position. The academic
ethic subdued the individual to moral norm, as to a higher
reality. The tragic poet, sensing confusion rather than asserting
clarity, appears to inquire after reality, and especially the reality
of the heroic person. "What amid all this is I?" is the question
constantly and poignantly arising from the pages of Sophocles.
The whole play, mounted with costume, mask, and music
against the stark Greek landscape, offered the spectator not doctrine, but a hypothesis of reality and identity, a myth of the
human condition rounded out by supporting symbols of language and spectacle, in which moral standards formed certainly
a part, but only a part, of the whole searching scheme. The
aim, in fact, was more metaphysical than strictly moral.

It may seem impossible for us, conditioned as we are by
analytic thought, to return to the states of mind of the Greeks
before Plato. They are doubtless only in part recoverable. An-
thropologists and folklorists find the original motifs of tragedy in
immemorial rituals that, even when they are not total inven-
tions, do not greatly enlighten our responses. Whatever the
function of the collective subconscious may be, it was probably
not so efficacious among the Athenian spectators as to take
precedence over the immediacy of the developed work of art
before them. Myth gathers meanings through time, and in its
fifth-century tragic form it would seem to reflect not the deaths

of Sacred Kings or Year Spirits, dimly recollected, if they ever existed, but the ever-present shape of mortality itself, the human condition viewed in the aspect of heroic extremes of action and aspiration.

There is a certain low brand of dramatic criticism, now fortunately on the wane, which offers solutions such as: If Oedipus had only controlled his temper better, he would not have come to grief; or, Othello could have saved himself a great deal of trouble if he had been less naive. These tasteless vulgarisms, which destroy the play rather than elucidate it, mark and intellectual nadir not, of course, to be identified with traditional ethical philosophy, but ultimately traceable to its influence. For traditional philosophy puts a veil between us and the hero in two ways· first, by substituting the moral mean for the heroic extreme as the meaningful focus of moral judgment; and second, by regarding man apart from the world of his responses, instead of as involved with it. For the hero is, indeed, an enlarged image of man, but still an image of man involved, and his involvement typifies every individual's involvement. It is of two kinds, outer and inner. His outward involvement with other men appears in the action of a tragedy; his inner involvement, being concerned chiefly with his intuition of a potential permanence, an absolute selfhood, is often partly adumbrated through "divine" symbols, such as oracles, curses, or epiphanies. These interlocking involvements, evident in varying forms throughout Greek heroic literature from Achilles on, constitute what might be called the paradox of the individual; raised to the heroic power, it becomes the tragic fatality which both exalts and destroys. Within this frame, moral values evolve and may become paramount, but it is, fundamentally, the frame that counts for the dramatic structure and meaning. Macbeth's moral history is neither edifying nor in need of dramatic representation; his involvements with his victims and with the witches reveal a mysterious paradigm of human experience.

The insufficiency of idealistic philosophy to deal with tragedy may be observed on many a page of classical criticism. Significantly, however, it was not idealism's literary insufficiency that prompted a different approach, but its insufficiency, as felt by Søren Kierkegaard in 1846, to answer the problem of the individual. With his usual abundance of stinging irony, Kierkegaard wrote in his *Concluding Unscientific Postscript* that the Hegelian system was a magnificent achievement, but with two faults: it never got finished, and it took no account of individual experience. The very fact of system became in itself a matter for protest unless it achieved the completeness it proposed; and Kierkegaard countered with the proposition that experience was best apprehended subjectively and "existentially," in a way that made truth itself subjective and system impossible. It is irrelevant here to debate the validity of Kierkegaard's dialectic, or to inquire how far Hegel himself, in the *Phenomenology of Mind*, had taken account of such an approach. In questioning the categories of idealistic philosophy, whose roots reached back to Socrates, Kierkegaard had opened the door simply and inevitably, though perhaps accidentally, upon states of consciousness that historically preceded the Socratic schools and had been obscured by them.

Numerous kinds of existentialism have arisen since Kierkegaard's original formulation; there is no one system. In American slang existentialism might be called a philosophical "do-it-yourself-kit." But there is a consistent approach, whose characteristics bear an extraordinary resemblance to the attitudes underlying ancient tragedy, those states of mind which, as said earlier, inhere in the symbols and myths of the tragic poet. It is as if these states of mind had lain for centuries under the tall structures of Aristotelian rationalism, waiting for a philosophy sufficiently akin to poetry to uncover them.

It may seem perverse to describe the attitudes of ancient tragedians in terms invented for the world of the Industrial Revolution, with its spiritual dismemberment, its technological progressivism, and its individual despair. Where in the placid world of Sophocles was there any room for *Angst*? The answer is, Everywhere. It is not merely that the age of Sophocles was in fact one of the most turbulent in history, as it ran through a series of wars from the Persian to the Peloponnesian; even more important were the social, political, and cultural upheavals which, by gradually wearing away the autonomy and authenticity of the individual, compelled a reassessment of the grand heroic assumptions inherited from Homer. The sophistic movement was in every way as disturbing as the Industrial Revolution. Different as they were, as phenomena, both enfeebled religion, both disintegrated the family, and both drove the thoughtful individual in quest of his own value.

For the Athenians of the mid–fifth century, the natural unit of thought was still the myth, or poetic symbol, with its syncretic qualities as described above. For Europeans of the mid–nineteenth century it was far otherwise, at least until Kierkegaard's effort provided a language for reality whose elements were similarly syncretic, wrought from the analogous cohesions of subjective and objective in experience. Reality, according to Kierkegaard, should not be looked upon as the given world of nature, nor should the human self be looked upon as a given, or preestablished, cognitive agent responding to the traditional categories of that world. Rather, reality, for human experience, was the immersion of the self in its world, whose categories could be understood only as modes of the self's immersion. Thus, "How am I involved in it?" and "How am I disposed toward it?" are the questions that reveal existential reality, not simply "What is it?" and "What am I?" as if the two were primarily discrete. From this point of view, existence, i.e., human existence, is regarded as prior to essential being, and this distinctly subjective mode of analysis is basic to all existential philosophy. Fact and response, or, in more technical terms, "facticity" and "affectivity," are in an empirical sense inseparable. The human creature is described as something hurled into a chaos of environment, out of which it can create order only by accepting, understanding, and responding to its own various involvements with that into which it is hurled. This is existence, in the most basic sense, and the question becomes, What can one do about it?

The answers are various, to say the least. For the deeply religious Kierkegaard, human existence leads inevitably through suffering and fear to the revelation of Christ; for Jean-Paul Sartre, it leads just as inevitably to atheism. Gabriel Marcel and Karl Jaspers have highly different focuses, while Martin Heidegger, who is the most relevant existentialist for Greek tragedy, seeks his answer through metaphysics. But if we look again for the common core, we find that all demand an arbitrary act of faith which each human being commits for himself, and for which he both creates and takes the responsibility. Thus it is a creative act, not an act of deductive reasoning, which lifts the human creature out of his anonymity, his mere existence, and makes him real. It is a choice, or commitment, which gives a man his claim to identity, and he must make it for himself. It was the very irrationality of the religious act of faith which made it true for Kierkegaard; *credo quia incredible est.* If it were rationally deducible, there would be no freedom or originality in the one thing man can give to God. Freedom and responsibility are indispensable tenets of existentialism, and yet one's freedom is founded on the necessity of binding oneself to a choice, or commitment. And herein, of course, one is reminded of St. Augustine's doctrine of free will: that man's will is free, but it is truly free only to seek God, for if it seeks anything else, it enslaves itself.

There are, certainly, important differences, especially in the work of atheistic existentialists, such as Sartre, for whom freedom has no point of divine absolute reference, as it did for Augustine, but is rather a continual process of choice and commitment. But the binding authority of the individual choice itself is common to both.

How does one come to this all-necessary choice, or commitment of faith? Here again, all existentialists take account of a

singular psychological phenomenon, first formulated and described by Kierkegaard in *Fear and Trembling* (1843), and
known technically as Dread (*Angst*). Unlike fear, which is the
fear of something, Dread is the dread of nothingness. It appears
as a kind of courage, a constant intuitive acknowledgment of the
rootlessness of mere existence. It is the call of the self to the self
not to be nothing. Heidegger calls this summons Conscience,
and he goes on to describe how it makes a man free to accept the
"guilt" of anonymity, the burden of his own nothingness, and
form a resolve, or commitment, by which he will make himself
something. Through the experience of this kind of Dread,
wherein one is threatened with total estrangement from himself,
the human creature makes the act of faith which creates and
constitutes his being. If he turns his back and flees from that
Dread of Nothingness, he becomes the pawn and toy of the
things that happen to him, and, worst of all, he does not even
know it. The whole phenomenon of Dread is not unlike what
William James called the process of being "twice-born"; it is the
consciousness of all things as they are for you, combined with
the acknowledgment of one's own responsibility to act and to
be.

Despite the grievous oversimplification of this outline, it may
permit us to see a little into the psychological structure of certain Greek tragic situations. In the earliest of the plays that
remain to us by Sophocles, the hero, Ajax, is introduced in a
state of madness. Disappointed that the famous armor of Achilles, now dead, has been awarded as prize to Odysseus and not to
himself, Ajax has attempted to murder the leaders of the Greek
host at Troy, but suddenly taking leave of his wits, has slain a
flock of sheep instead. Odysseus, his enemy, watches him with
some anxiety from a safe distance, and then, with a sudden
surge of pity and recognition, says:

> I see that we are nothing other than
> Images, we who live, or weightless shadow.
>
> [125f.]

The intuition of human life as nothingness, appearing here in the prologue of the play, lays the ground bass for the scenes that follow. Ajax has become transparent, a ghostly mockery of himself, and Odysseus, beholding him thus, sees all lives as "weightless shadow," mere images. It is an experience of Dread, and when Ajax comes to himself, he too experiences it. After his first laments, he looks around for himself, and cannot find anywhere the self that he would recognize. The ancient heroes enjoyed a vast native self-respect on the whole, a self-respect that rested on birth, tradition, valor, and, above all, self-discipline. The insanity of Ajax, by suspending his self-discipline, has destroyed his self-respect, and in a way his very reality. One must assume that in former times he had reality; his exploits, positive acts of valor done after some fashion for their own sakes, had afforded him an eminent solidity in his own eyes and in the eyes of all. Now all this has been swept away in the surge of madness wherein he has totally lost himself and become the tool of the invisible force of unreason. There is no suggestion that insanity condones his action. The madness itself, sent by Athena, is the mockery and provokes the challenge. Reduced to nothing, Ajax must recreate himself, prove that he still is himself, and the means to this end can be found only in action. He asks himself what he will now do, and after rejecting various alternatives, concludes darkly:

> Find some such enterprise
> Whereby I may reveal to my old father
> That I, his son, am not of nature mean.
> [470ff.]

Physis, essential nature, seeks a positive act in which to vindicate iteself permantly and undeniably as being. And this search is what the existentialists call the act of Care (*Sorge*). Ajax's answer, suicide, may seem hardly a positive act; rather, a negative one. Why must it be death? Ajax is given the alternative of patience, with redemption in time. His responsibility to his friends and dependents is powerfully urged by his concubine Tecmessa and by the chorus. Yet his rejection of these possibilities in the play appears as inevitable—at least to those who have not adopted the stand that all virtue resides in moderation. If the real issue is the ultimate one of being, it must have an ultimate answer. Ajax chooses death because he wills to complete himself, and not to allow the mockery of the divine being Athena, or even the quiet observation of Odysseus, to be the final word. He will offer a self-completed Ajax to the scrutiny of posterity. Sophocles clearly means his decision to have its desired effect. As he stands by the body at the end, Odysseus, having secured honorable burial for his enemy, estimates him now somewhat differently:

> This man was once, of all the army, most
> My enemy, since I won Achilles' arms;
> Such though he was to me, I would not so
> Dishonor him in turn as to deny
> He was the greatest of the Argives, all
> Of us who came to Troy, except Achilles.
> [1336ff.]

When a man's honor and value are defended by his worst enemy in such terms, the matter is closed, in drama at least. Ajax has won his case. He is dead, he is a ghost indeed; but he is not a "weightless shadow." He has given his life reality again, by the self-conscious discipline of his departure from it. And the majestic funeral march that closes the play formally betokens the final engagement of a magnanimous individual with the universe.

In the philosophy of Heidegger, death is called the "innermost and absolute potentiality of being." To define it so is, of course, to regard death as not merely the end of physical life, but the completion of spiritual life. The tragic hero, therefore, when he takes his own life, asserts correspondingly not merely his independence of the physical, but his control of the spiritual life, in the structural aspect of its entirety. The experience of Dread followed by Care, it has been observed, builds the individual while it destroys his finiteness; and death, insofar as it destroys the finite life of man, is similar in its dramatic function here. Ajax all but says explicitly that he will have no more to do with the world of time, whose shifts and changes he recounts with irony and sorrow, in some of Sophocles' most beautiful lines (669ff.). But existence is penetrated through and through by time, and if real being is to be timeless, the only way to reach it is by leaving existence, that is, by dying.

Herein we undoubtedly read the real meaning and effect of the deaths that so frequently bring tragedies to a close. Whether or not every man chooses his own death, the tragic hero certainly does. For the tragic hero, at least in Greek drama, death is simply the final stage of his own self-formation, which the rest of the play has revealed. In Sophocles in particular, the hero's effort is all toward giving his life a spiritual content and ontological structure that will be ratified in his death; and the process is not very different from what Heidegger calls the "Being-toward-Death," or the orientation of one's temporal existence with full acknowledgment that its most absolute potentiality is death, and that it may therefore, by conscience and foresight, be treated in advance as a whole. Socrates himself said nothing so very different when he remarked that a philosopher's whole life is a preparation for death.

The dramatization of such peculiarly inward, individual problems is characteristic of the theater of Sophocles, as we know it, in the second half of the fifth century. For Aeschylus, the poet of the previous, less fragmented generation, the question of individual authenticity had not yet taken such acute form. Yet in the *Prometheus* there is a distinct hint that the Being-toward-Death is a basic creative function of the human creature. Prometheus, chained by Zeus to a crag in the

Caucasus for the theft of fire, indignantly protests his treatment and recounts to the chorus all the benefits the possession of fire made possible for mankind—architecture, metal-work, agriculture, divination, all the arts and crafts, which the Greeks called *technai*. The chorus leader then asks if he did not do something else that might have prompted Zeus to such a cruel revenge. "Yes," he replies; "I prevented mortals from foreseeing their deaths." "How?" asks the chorus. "By planting blind hopes in their hearts." "A handsome benefit," says the chorus vaguely (247ff.). The passage is conspicuous by reason of its apparent irrelevance amid the material, technological blessings resulting from fire. Yet, when it has been noticed at all by commentators, it is simply added in with Prometheus's other gifts as a good thing. But the opposite may be the truth, and if so, then Prometheus perhaps should not be looked upon as simply the benign philanthropist suffering martyrdom at the hands of brute, jealous power. It seems odd, for instance, that a divinity whose name means "forethought" should deprive mortals of the foresight of their own most absolute potential, while endowing them with the advantages of science. What is Aeschylus saying? Does material progress come at the price of having blind, unlimited expectations, instead of foreknowledge of one's own structure and limitation? In our own time we have found that to be very much the case, and it would appear that Aeschylus also had some such feeling in mind, confronted by the fifth century's ever-advancing imperialism and materialism, which, if not quite an industrial revolution, nonetheless were transforming Athenian life, and were promising to be limitless. The *Prometheus* may well be as late as 457 or 456 B.C.; if so, it falls in the year that witnessed Athens' first overt attempt to dominate Greece by force of arms and wealth, the beginning of those imperialistic moves that prompted Pindar to write a decade later the somewhat Sophoclean line: "What is man? The dream of a shadow" (*Pythian* 8. 95–96).

We do not know how the *Prometheus* trilogy ended, save that

the Titan was at last released and reconciled with Zeus. But it is
clear that the tragic tension was kept alive through another,
similar withholding of foreknowledge. Prometheus had declared
that Zeus would marry a goddess whose son was to be greater
than his father, but he refused to say which goddess. Since we
have only the first play of the three, it is impossible to trace
definitely the significance or exact outcome of this stalemate,
but it seems inescapable that here, again, Prometheus's action is
contrary to his appropriate function. His previous statement
about preventing men from foreseeing their fate contrasts with
his prophecy to Io of her future sufferings, and also with the
chorus's remark that it is good to know one's adversities in
advance (698f.). It seems not impossible that, in Aeschylus's
eyes, Prometheus, for all his benign intention, was misled in
giving science and blind hope and suppressing foreknowledge
of limit and spiritual potential. The first commandment of
Delphic wisdom was "Know thyself," which meant, "Know that
you are mortal." If the condition of Prometheus's philanthropy
was to contravene this basic law, there would seem to be a clear
case of a mess of pottage for a birthright. To know that you are
mortal is to be able to Be-toward-Death, and to preserve that
state of Care by which one shapes one's life inwardly. The
Prometheus seems to be saying that the human creature grows
by the exercise of spirit, not by the calculations of science. Such
a view is certainly characteristic of existentialism, which revolts,
if not against science itself, at least against the imposition of
exact scientific method on all life. If the foregoing analysis has
any truth in it, then the *Prometheus* would emerge as the earliest protest against the similar reduction of the spirit between
the mill wheels of Athenian progressivism and the systematic
sophistic calculus.

As said earlier, the problem of individual characters' authentication does not arise in Aeschylus in so central a fashion as in
Sophocles. Yet it appears in other ways, as when, for instance,
the total action of a play becomes identified with the main

figure at a climactic point. Here a catalytic symbol is necessary to express the crisis in the individual life, and Aeschylus has recourse to the supernatural. When Eteocles in the *Seven against Thebes* cries, "The hostile black curse of my father sits upon me with hard, unweeping eyes," he identifies himself in a new way (695f.). Hitherto, he has stood for reason and the steady, firm direction of his city under stress; but now the moment of real action has come, and his decision to post himself against his brother at the seventh gate is called for neither by reason nor by strategy. It is prompted by hate, or perhaps better, by the whole nexus of passions that have been operative in the family for three generations. Here Eteocles drops the mask of reason and let us see in action who he is, a man demonically possessed, and fully as accursed as the hated brother whom he is going out to slay. Similarly, but even more explicitly, in the *Agamemnon*, Clytemnestra, after announcing that she has murdered her husband, says to the chorus:

> You aver this deed is mine;
> But do not think
> Me Agamemnon's wife.
> Likening himself to this dead man's wife
> The ancient bitter Fury
> Of Atreus, merciless banquet-giver,
> Has requited him,
> Adding an adult sacrifice to that of the young.
> [1497ff.]

Here the identification is as complete as possible: Clytemnestra, her action, the Fury (*alastor*) of the house of Atreus, all the ancient crimes and their motivating passions are caught in a moment of totally, if criminally, realized selfhood. The chorus thinks that she is trying to disclaim responsibility for her crime, but quite the opposite (cf. 1404ff.); she is identifying herself with it and with the Fury. Clytemnestra has veiled herself carefully before; now she tells us who she is.

Such moments may seem far removed from the process of Ajax's spiritual self-redemption. It might be difficult to discover in Clytemnestra the solemn mystery of Dread, or the moral decisiveness of Care. Authentication of a sort is here, but the authenticating action appears to be only partly chosen; it is also in part imposed by the passionate web of demonic drives. Clytemnestra and Eteocles are caught; Ajax has eluded capture. Yet one sees in Aeschylus the basis from which the Sophoclean vision could grow: the involvement of the actor in the action and the consequent doubt about the reality of the self. Is it Clytemnestra, or is it the Fury? And whichever it is, what is either without the other? For Sophocles, a generation later, the problem could be looked upon differently: the fatal involvement (*Verworfenheit*) of man could not be remedied; it was the condition of all, whether one acted or not, whence perhaps the saying "Not to be born is best." But the acceptance of this fact could be made clearer in the individual soul. Also, choice, though it could lead the external man into a deadly web of action, might so legislate for the inward man that the latter could emerge self-wrought and pure, bound, no doubt, to circumstances, action, and consequence, but redeemed and liberated by the inner structures of moral self-command and lofty motive. Such a concept, based on the discrepancies of outer versus inner, visible versus invisible, led inevitably to the famous "isolated hero" of Sophoclean tragedy: others see the hero's fate; the hero sees himself. Hence, too, the ironies of knowledge and circumstance breed and proliferate. In the early plays, the difference between the hero himself, the choosing agent, and the results of his choice are fatal; only death can clarify the inner moral structures of Ajax, Antigone, Deianeira. The later heroes exercise greater inward freedom by combining a further acceptance of circumstance with a further lonely insistence on choice and motive. These are the pariahs, Electra, Philoctetes, and Oedipus, who somehow live so exclusively by their own spirits that the fates that have forced them to such a state become in turn the modes and means of their self-authentication. In them, mastery and acceptance are one. What has happened is that the tragic dilemma has come full circle, from the dread that individual being is impossible in the chaos of existence, to the conviction that only from the chaos of existence can individual being be created.

Greek tragedy and existentialism both take root in the soil of despair; both emphasize suffering, yet both militantly declare the power of the human spirit to rescue itself from anonymity and assert its being. For both, being is a moral achievement, a lifting by one's own bootstraps, based on the knowledge that life is, to begin with, meaningless. In both, the first prompting to such creativity of the self is the intuition of nothingness, Dread, the call of the self to the self; for both, the process is complete only with death, though a man may achieve a potential wholeness and integrity through a foreknowing acceptance of death. An explicit statement of such consciousness is found in the *Oedipus at Colonus*, where Theseus, after referring to himself as "a stranger and a nothingness," says to the aged, dying Oedipus:

> Being a man, I know that I possess
> No greater share of tomorrow than you do.
>   [567f.]

How frequent it is, especially in Sophocles, to find the tragic hero calling himself a "nothing"! How near the surface always is that bleak knowledge of rootlessness which is the essence of tragic suffering. Less bitter, in a way, to Oedipus are the things that happened to him than the knowledge that he is that to which anything can happen. But that is precisely what he is, the man who, despite every effort to live uprightly, found that he had committed parricide and incest without knowing it. But Sophocles does not stop with the helplessness of Oedipus. Shattered though he is, Oedipus continues to live; his moral integ-

rity has made him free, as Heidegger might say, for "guilt," that
is, free and able to bear his own weightlessness, his own nothingness. Unlike Ajax, he accepts these terms, perhaps with even
greater courage, until, on the last day of his life, as he feels his
deification coming upon him, he say say: "When I am nothing,
then am I a man?" (393). Somehow, the sheer tugging at the
bootstraps has worked. In classical times, Oedipus was worshiped near Athens as a demigod.

Sophocles was the last of the Greek tragedians to conceive
tragedy in such a wise. Euripides seldom drew such full
philosophic portraits of human nature, but was rather given to
the smaller emotional and psychological elements that go to
make it up. He is concerned with such themes as selfishness,
lust, brutality, and prudishness, but seldom with a metaphysical, or mythic, conception of human character. The result is
that his tragedies take the shape, as a rule, of the decay and fall
of the human spirit, rather than of its triumph through self-
authentication, though the three late "romances" are important
exceptions. One reason for this is that he sometimes joined the
rationalists in attacking myth, and it was from myth that generations of Greeks had derived their concept of personality. Myth is
history, conceived not as fact, but as existence completed and
relived. It is the shape of life rounded with meaning, and its
function is to reveal life, or some aspect of it, in greater totality
than one can experience in temporal, day-by-day existence.
One might call it a vision of timeless being; and by constantly
referring their lives to their myths, the earlier Greeks afforded
themselves that power of spiritual extension, of projection of the
self onto the large canvas of the universe in general, which has
made Greek art of all kinds so irreplaceable. Myth has never
entirely ceased to function in the life of Greece, and certain
Greek writers today employ it with nearly the same subtlety and
freshness as did their illustrious ancestors. But there have been
periods when it was less meaningful, and the generation of
Euripides was one. Greece was preparing to give birth to philos-

ophy; the young Plato was listening to Socrates, and the new product was destined to supplant the old mythic way of thinking and conceiving life. Perhaps for this reason Euripides' characters lack the dimension of self-determination that those of Sophocles have. They are pawns, "weightless shadow," and in their petty concerns they embody what some existentialists call the "estrangement from the self." To borrow once more a phrase of Heidegger's, they are "caught in the world of their care," involved not in time as a whole, or in the Being-toward-Death, but in their own little presents; they do not fall, like heroes, against the enlarging vistas of man's being; they spin down pathetically like dry leaves in the autumn, examples of the nothingness of existence, not of men whose choice has freed or redeemed them. Thus Pentheus in the *Bacchae*, the victim of a punily conceived moral duty, is torn to pieces by his own mother and her frenzied associates; or the tormented Hecuba, when Troy has fallen, is so maddened by her sufferings and thirst for vengeance that she becomes indeed a mad and screaming female hound. In such a kind of tragedy, one may justifiably see a closer analogy to French than to German existentialism; in France there is a tendency to emphasize the meaningless ground of existence; in Germany, the potentiality of moral structure and authentic being.

A full exposition of what the existentialists mean by self-authentication would be lengthy. Choice, or the act of faith which is the creative expression of the human creature's wish for reality, has already been mentioned. It comes in part as a concomitant of that Dread, which, it must be remembered, is not the same as fear, but stands, as Heidegger says, "in secret union with the serenity and gentleness of creative longing." He describes it also as a kind of "spellbound peace," in which the phenomenal world is revealed in all its nothingness, so that the possibility of real Being may appear. Such an experience is indeed a profound psychic state, but it should not be confused with mysticism, for in it one communes only with oneself.

Heidegger's description of it prompts a comparison with the ineffable self-containment and world-awareness of the Athenian grave-steles of the fifth century. These do not express human life in full transcendence, as do, say, Rafael's madonnas, but they embody the quiet, spiritual watchfulness in which transcendence is implied. They seem to be waiting for something in the midst of nothing. They are, in fact, bas-reliefs of Dread. But self-authentication does not stop with Dread; free choice, the act of faith, Care, and finally sacrifice must enter, before the human condition can transcend its mere existence and be. It is here, perhaps, that the existentialist views are least worked out and most contradictory about what moral content, if any, the choice must have. For Sartre, apparently, any choice, so long as it be chosen, is sufficient. But there should, it seems, be moral content in the choice, and the existentialists have not agreed what the moral contents should be. In the present context, Heidegger's doctrine of sacrifice is the most promising. For Heidegger, as perhaps for Augustine, the only really free choice is sacrifice, of one's self, of course, because this alone, as he says, "expends itself in Being for the truth of Being." All other choices are mere calculations, necessary all the time, but of no import for self-authentication. Again, Heidegger says, "Sacrifice brooks no calculation;" the "spirit of sacrifice . . . takes upon itself Kinship with the imperishable," a phrase reminiscent of Kierkegaard's "Making the motions of Eternity." Here again, one is reminded of Sophocles. Ajax's death is a sacrifice by which he takes upon himself "Kinship with the imperishable." It is his declaration of moral freedom from the circumstances and events that have overwhelmed him. So too with Antigone, whose choice brings foreseen death. So too with Oedipus. He cannot ignore the crimes that he has discovered he committed; he must do something, and he chooses to sacrifice his eyesight. "Apollo destroyed me," he cries, "but I struck this blow" (1329ff.); meaning that his self-blinding is a freely offered token of the moral integrity he wills in contrast to the circum-

stances that have ruined him. Tragic suffering is always, in
Sophocles, a sacrifice by the hero to the being he conceives
himself to be. Thereby he transcends his mere existence, and
merges, as it were, with that larger, mythic self with which
Greek heroic tradition provided him. Antigone may never, in
fact, have existed, but she is more real than most people who
have.

To call *Oedipus Rex* a study in the search for the self is
nothing new, and to describe it in existentialist terms may seem
to be wayward and profitless. Yet, by this road one may elude
the moral terms devised by Plato, for whom tragedy was a fascinating cultural mistake; and there may be other advantages.
Tragic thinking and existential thinking seem both to have been
necessitated, at least in part, by a concern for the individual in
his metaphysical aspect. If the existentialist concern arose from
the shipwreck of the individual in nineteenth-century Europe,
one may justifiably see in Antigone a comparable foundering of
the personal life before the frozen statecraft of Creon. Intuitions
of Being and Nothing, integrity and helplessness, choice and
fatality are basic to both the existentialists and the tragedians.
The paradox of greatness-in-smallness shines through both. For
Kierkegaard, the "humblest" thing a man can do is take a stand
before God. Oedipus, who, in his lofty determination toward
innocence, measured his course from Corinth "by the stars," is
measured at last by the length of a brooch-pin, the one thing he
can command. Yet Oedipus stands.

The heroic and the existential have their kinship, but there
are also important differences. The problem of the individual
was not identical in both periods, by any means. More important, ideas such as freedom, choice, or sacrifice may have
needed reintroduction into modern Europe, but they were always natives of Greece. The poets of the great classical tradition
found these issues to be the basic ones as naturally as they found
air breathable. A man must ask himself who he is and in what
quarter he may expect to discover the meaning and reality of his

life. We are born to a general anonymity, but we seek something better by giving our particular its due of genuine selfhood,
which will also, however, be a universal. Our being is a being-
in-the-world, and our selfhood cannot be something divorced
from it. As early as Homer, one finds a clear statement of the
problem of anonymity versus selfhood in the famous speech of
Glaucus to Diomedes in the sixth book of the *Iliad:*

As of the leaves, so also is the generation of men:
Some of the leaves the wind scatters on earth, but others the forest
Flourishing breeds, and the season of spring comes on.
So of men, one generation grows, another fades...

[6. 146ff.]

He then, however, recounts his own ancestry, slowly par-
ticularizing himself from history, till he comes to his own acceptance of the heroic heritage, "Always to be valorous, and
superior to others" (208)—from the leaflike nothingness of passing existence, to the moral espousal of the warrior's faith, with
its uncalculating sacrifice of smaller self-conceptions, and its
"kinship with the imperishable."

It is interesting to see the existentialists working slowly back
through complex philosophic paths to states of mind that existed
so naturally and simply in pagan Greece. Before the advent of
revealed religion, before the advent even of philosophy, such
attitudes are inevitably bound to arise, although they do not
receive any special name. They are based on a simple
phenomenology of human experience, and they express themselves most naturally in poetry. Prose is the language of systematic philosophy, and when the latter was born in Greece, Greek
classical poetry faded. But systems, as Kierkegaard knew,
though they have elegance of their own, and theoretical truth,
do not supplant the chaos of the actual. At most they can clarify
part of it. Yet chaos is there for the individual to find his way
through, and, like Aphrodite from the sea, poetry rises from

chaos. Greek poetry went on being written, and is still being
written, holding steadily the course of its grand tradition. It is
the thread of this tradition, with its unmediated directness of
human response, and its center lying firmly in the moral, or
better, sacrificial, act of individual faith, which existentialism is
seeking. Both Heidegger and Kierkegaard have written on
poetry, and Kierkegaard in particular was fascinated by heroism,
freedom, and sacrifice. Surely, so far as these two greatest existentialists are concerned, their search was for just so genuinely
humanistic an outlook as we have tried to trace in Sophocles,
and somewhat in Aeschylus. Existentialism is sometimes dis-
missed as mere atheism and decadence; rather, its point of departure is pagan, and its achievement may yet be, when it is
further worked out, a regenerated classicism, not in the
academic sense, but in the rediscovery of motive forces underlying classical Greek literature, and hence our whole civilization.
Something of this must have been understood by Heidegger,
who, in his essay "What Is Metaphysics?" quotes the closing
lines of Sophocles' *Oedipus at Colonus* as a token of what he
calls the Greeks' "entry into the mysterious truth of Being."

3. Association by Theme in the *Iliad*

Almost two centuries have passed since there appeared in Europe a book on Homer which shook to its roots every previously held belief about The Poet, as he was called in antiquity, and sparked a new era of debate about the authorship and composition of the *Iliad* and the *Odyssey*. The book was F. A. Wolf's *Prolegomena ad Homerum*, published in 1795, in which the great scholar declared that the two epics were composed years before the introduction of writing into Greece, and that therefore (1) they, with their tremendous bulk, could not have been created, and retained by memory, in the mind of a single poet; and (2) they must therefore represent the conglomerate efforts of many bards, later assembled, rather haphazardly, into the poems we know. The debate, which lasted over a century and is still going on to a degree, arose between the so-called Unitarians, who clung to the vision of one inspired poet, and the Analysts, or Divisionists, who found everywhere the traces of many hands of exceedingly disparate competence; the countless writings on both sides of the question failed to prove whether Homer was one or many, though they did prove that the combatants were fertile with invective. The Unitarians rebuked the Analysts for cold-blooded dissection of the poems and lack of literary sensitivity, while the Analysts sneered at the Unitarians for romantic naiveté. By the beginning of the twentieth century, the Analysts by and large had the upper hand—though it is hard to say which Analyst, for each divided the poems against themselves in a different way, each with his own criteria for what was "genuine and old" versus what was "late and corrupt," but all of them glorying triumphantly over such few Unitarians as still lurked cowering, mostly in America, treasuring their faith in the integrity of Homer and his two long-admired masterpieces. We now know that Wolf was right in thinking that the Homeric poems were created without the use of writing; we also know, as he did not, that one man *can* make a poem the length of the *Iliad* or the *Odyssey*. There is much that remains mysterious about the actual process of composition, but we are beginning to understand that oral poets, or singers—for musical accompaniment played an important part—approach the task of composition in a way quite different from the literate poet, and therefore they demand of the hearer, reader, or critic a different kind of criticism, a new poetics, with different presuppositions about unity, structure, and relevance.

What we know about the composition of oral poetry we have learned primarily from the work of Milman Parry, the other great revolutionist in modern Homeric scholarship.[1] Even as a student in Paris in the twenties, and before his famous fieldwork in Yugoslavia in the early thirties, Parry was convinced that the language of Homer was a traditional language with a history of many centuries before Homer used it, and that it was constructed largely out of "formulaic" elements, words or groups of words identified with certain metrical sections of the dactylic line, which the poet could call upon as he needed them in creating his verses.

Later, in order to get a view of the process at first hand, Parry went to Yugoslavia with a tape recorder and there collected a large number of oral epic songs performed by illiterate singers

---

1. [Parry's work is conveniently available in *The Making of Homeric Verse: The Collected Papers of Milman Parry*, ed. Adam Parry (Oxford, 1971).]

nurtured in the Serbo-Croatian tradition. Thus he could offer an analogue in a living language to the technique that Homer, in his belief, followed. Most of the poems were short, only a few hundred lines, but eventually Parry found a singer, named Avdo Međedović, who could sing a really long poem, an epic of 12,000 lines, in fact, or about the same length as the *Odyssey*. But Međedović did not sing it from memory; he composed it on the spot—or rather, recomposed, for Avdo Međedović had sung it before, numerous times. But he made this especially elaborate version to please Parry, and Parry recorded it.

All this did not, of course, prove that the epics of Homer were the work of a single poet—though Parry himself, an ardent Unitarian, believed that. It did prove, however, that a single poet *could* have created them, and thus for all time rescued the Unitarians from the contumelious shadow under which the brilliance of the Analysts' "Higher Criticism" had thrust them. But more interesting, perhaps, was the insight that such research provided into the way oral poets worked, the constraints that are brought to bear upon them in the actual process of performing a traditional song, their manner of constructing the poems that they sing, and the slips and inconsistencies that they commit. A great new light fell on all the discrepancies and apparent irrelevancies that for decades had led scholars to the conclusion that the *Iliad* was a pastiche, and not a very clever one.

Yet all this new knowledge brought its problems, as new knowledge usually does. Parry, who died in 1935 at the age of thirty-three, left much to his successors in the way of framing critical approaches to the *Iliad* and *Odyssey* as oral poems. To many it seemed that oral composition was a merely mechanical process, that the charge of illiteracy was an affront to the "Prince of Poets," as George Chapman called him, and that Parry had gone even further than Wolf in denying Homer any genius at all. Some have recoiled so violently that they insist that Homer, however he may have used an oral tradition, himself had a pen and wrote the *Iliad*, for otherwise it could never have been so good; others have felt that Homer must have used at least notes—a professorial assumption. Parry's ghost must walk and wring its hands at such compromising partiality to the art of writing, which even Plato called overrated. There are cogent reasons for believing that Homer as an oral poet, though writing existed in his own day, could not—or better would not—have ever thought of making use of it. But more important, it should be recognized that oral composition is very far from being a mechanical process, that illiteracy is no handicap to a poet well versed in a traditional mode of storytelling, and that genius, always mysterious and never quite within a critic's grasp, fulfills itself in ways that cannot be prescribed, and must, if possible, be simply followed. Our aim should be to see a little into the workings of the Homeric mind, to describe its freedom of movement within the tradition, and to observe some of the ways by which Homer, that supreme illiterate, arrived at the wonderful dramatic structure and poetic texture of the *Iliad*.

We said that Homer's poetry was "formulaic," as well as traditional. To say that makes it sound as if everything Homer said had been said before—which is precisely the case, and must be granted, if we reckon squarely with the nature and function of an inherited poetic tradition. What, therefore, is remarkable about the *Iliad*, least of all unique? Surely there must be something special about it, something peculiarly the poet's own, to account for the fact that it, and it alone, save for its sister poem, the *Odyssey*, was selected out of all the poems in the rich Greek heroic heritage to be recorded—by whatever means it was recorded—and preserved. Even as the older, Divisionist scholars looked for what was "genuine and old" in the poems, so now many younger scholars today are seeking what is "original," versus "traditional," Homer's own contribution to the lore he inherited from the immemorial past. But such efforts are disappointing in the very degree to which they are subjective. It is futile to seize upon some striking lines or phrases and claim

that they are Homer's own creation amid all that is formulaic,
when we have no idea how many epics there may have been
before Homer in which the same passages might have occurred.
Though everything must have an origin, in the case of Greek
epic poetry we are in no position to say what the origin of any
element may have been. But there is another reason for not
looking for Homer's originality of phrase or line, a more positive
reason, which may bring us one step closer to what Homer
actually was doing. This reason is: Oral poets do not aim at
originality. The whole distinction between "original" and "traditional," which is so fundamental to our critical thinking, is
wholly foreign to a bard who composes poems in his head for a
listening audience. As we know from Parry and Lord's fieldwork
in Yugoslavia, the standard claim of such a bard is that he sings
the song exactly as he learned it. The fact that the claim is not
literally true does not matter; it indicates the poet's attitude, and
his standard of excellence. He is the preserver of a tradition he
reveres as true, and he harbors no ambition to improve upon it.
The self-conscious ego of the "creative artist" casts neither light
nor shadow on the work that he performs; and it is of great
importance to our critique of Homer to reflect that with him it
must have been the same.

And yet here we must pause: The oral poet does not, in fact,
sing the song just as he learned it. Parry's collection contains a
great many recordings of the same poem as sung by different
poets, and of the same poem as sung by the same poet on
different occasions, and no two are alike. The bard only thinks
that he always produces the same performance. He uses the
same scenario, the same formalized language, the same characters. But the arrangement and development of scenes, the
choice of formulas, the inclusion or exclusion of details (sometimes crucial ones), the ornamentation by way of similes and
the like, and hence the very length of the poem—all these differ
from bard to bard, and from performance to performance. And
to trace out *these* differences is to see where the poet's taste, or

whimsy, leads him, and to see something of his work as an artist.

Now, is it possible, one may fairly ask, that a bard can make all these changes and not be aware of them? This is a delicate point. The bard claims he always sings the song the same way, but he also knows he sings it better than another bard—or, less frequently, the reverse. Furthermore, if really pressed, he may admit that he can sing it better than he just did. As Homer's near contemporary Hesiod remarked, "Bard envies bard" (*Works and Days* 26); and, of course, prizes in antiquity were given in contests to the best singer. The variations, then, are there, and the singer is aware of them, though they seem never to be his primary concern. To him, the song is all traditional, and he will render it as best he can; but what actually comes to the listener each time is a new, original performance, which he judges, as one judges all performances, by its effectiveness. As Michael Nagler has phrased it: "All is traditional on the generative level, all original on the level of performance."[2]

We are concerned, then, with *variations*, but not variations as indications of any antinomy between "original" and "traditional," but rather as tokens of Homer's way of telling the story of the anger of Achilles. Besides variations thematic associations are particularly revealing as evidence for the workings of the poet's mind. For patterns of association are uniquely a poet's own, and while the language of a poem, the characters in it, and the outline of the story are all "given" by tradition, his personal acceptance of these will make itself manifest in the arrangement of his episodes (to greater or lesser dramatic effect), in the individual coloring of his characters, and in the choice and timing of his use of traditional elements in the language, so that they achieve high poetic resonance, as well as decorum.

One simple example of the use of traditional elements is the

2. Michael Nagler, *Spontaneity and Tradition: A Study in the Oral Art of Homer* (Berkeley and Los Angeles, 1974), p. 26.

simile of a star. Numerous things in the *Iliad* are compared to
stars—campfires, a beautiful robe, the infant Astyanax. The
comparison of a hero's flashing bronze armor to a star is natural
and expectable, and we may contrast two occasions when
Homer uses it. In Book 5, he says of Diomedes in arms:

> From his helm and shield unwearying fire flashed,
> Like the autumn star that most of all
> Shines brightly, washed in the waters of Ocean.
>
> > [5. 3–6]

The autumn star is Sirius, of course, the brightest of all the fixed
stars. In Book 22, Achilles' arms are also compared to it, but
details are now added which alter its nature and make the effect
quite different:

> Priam was first to see him with his eyes,
> Rushing over the plain, gleaming like a star,
> The star that comes in autumn, and its brilliant rays
> Flash among the many stars in the darkness of night;
> It is the star they call Dog of Orion.
> Brightest it is, and a sign of evil,
> And it brings much fever to suffering mortals...
>
> > [22. 25–31]

In Diomedes' star, the emphasis had been simply on supreme
brightness; Diomedes is a plain fellow, cheerfully courageous
on the field and a luminary among fighters. Achilles' star,
though it's the same one, is prophetic of evil, as laden with
tragic import as is Achilles himself, as he races forward to slay
Hector and prepare for the fall of Troy. A deeper vein of association has been tapped for Achilles' star, and the difference in the
handling of a quite traditional comparison reinforces the difference between the two heroes as Homer has conceived them
and their roles in the poem.

Another slightly more complex example again involves a
simile. In Book 2 Agamemnon, having just been sent from

Zeus a deceitful dream that he will be able to capture Troy that very day, makes an address to the troops. Instead of telling them about the encouraging dream, he does the opposite, and, pretending despair, he proposes to raise the siege and go home:

> Friends, heroes, Danaoi, companions of Ares,
> Zeus, son of Kronos, has bound me to a heavy doom,
> Wretch that he is, who first promised me, bowing his head,
> That I should sack Troy with its great walls, and return home,
> But now has contrived vile deceit, and bids me
> Homeward inglorious to Argos, now that I have lost many men.
> So, I suppose, all along it was the decision of almighty Zeus,
> Who has shattered the tops of many cities,
> And yet will shatter . . .
>
> [2. 110–18]

Agamemnon is lying, as Zeus lied to him. The troops do not know what he is up to—and neither do most of the commentators, but that is another question, irrelevant here. Seven books later, at the beginning of Book 9, Agamemnon repeats these words, in the longest consecutive repetition in the *Iliad*, if one leaves out messages repeated verbatim by the messenger. The second passage must be meant to recall the first, for the words are identical; or perhaps the first is meant to foreshadow the second. The king's feigned despair of Book 2 becomes real despair in Book 9, after the defeat Hector has inflicted on the Achaeans in the brief battle of Book 8; and this real despair is expressed in his burst of weeping, which is adorned by a simile:

> Agamemnon
> Stood up, pouring tears "like a spring of dark water,
> That pours its black waters down from a steep cliff."
> So, deeply groaning, he addressed the Argives.
>
> [9. 113–16]

He then repeats his suggestion to give up and flee; but the passage, now that the despair is genuine, is colored by a vivid

simile; it is marked, as it were, by a tragic asterisk, for fuller
attention.

Homer has not finished with this growing cluster of related
elements. At the beginning of Book 16, a book that shows a
symmetry with Book 9 both in its numerical position and in its
contents,[3] Patroclus comes to Achilles to beg him either to
relent and help the hard-pressed Greeks or to lend his arms and
send him, Patroclus, forth to their rescue. Patroclus in his turn
is in tears, and Homer repeats the simile of the dark-watered
spring word for word. But we know, and the ancient audiences
knew, that Patroclus is about to go forth to his death, so the
blackness of the spring's waters now betokens not only the defeat
of the Achaeans, but the death of Achilles' dearest friend, and
the fatal necessity for Achilles to avenge him, and himself per-
ish. Lest anyone miss that point, Homer says openly that Patroclus was a fool and was asking for his own destruction. Add to
that the fact that the blackness of the water and the steepness of
the cliff over which it pours both recall two frequent epithets for
death, "black" and "steep," and we see that Homer can do, by
association, repetition, and elaboration, to make his traditional
medium rich and telling. The elements in this series are all
traditional, including the leader's quite conventional proposal
of flight; but Homer has transformed them into a deepening
tragic progression, from pretended despair (no simile), to real
despair (simile of dark-watered spring), to tragic irony (that
simile in a new and deepened meaning).

Presently we shall see how this kind of association seems to
have contributed to the architectonics of the *Iliad* as a whole.
But first, let's look at one more example of simple enrichment,
this time by the inclusion of details that might be considered
superfluous, or even quite irrelevant. Granted that the events of
his poem and the language in which it was told were in some
sense fixed and preordained by tradition, yet the poet was free to

3.   [See Whitman, *Homer and the Heroic Tradition*, pp. 279–83.]

omit or include, as his own taste, or the pressures of time, might dictate. Homer's omissions would make an interesting study; but here we have to deal with something included, and for reasons not immediately apparent. Toward the end of Book 11, Achilles sees a wounded warrior being carried out of the battle in the chariot of Nestor, and he sends Patroclus to find out who it is. Arrived at the tent of Nestor, Patroclus sees that the wounded man is Machaon, son of Asclepius and principal surgeon of the Greek army, and is about to hurry back to Achilles with that information. But Nestor detains him, rather typically, with a long story about himself and then with an appeal to Patroclus either to rouse Achilles from his angry retirement or to borrow his arms and help the Greeks himself. In a striking passage, Nestor points out that Achilles' greatness will be of no use to anyone but himself if he goes on in this way, and contrasts his own valor, which he, when young, had devoted to the service of his fellow men (11. 658–803). Patroclus is moved by this argument, which neatly pinpoints what is probably the most central issue of the *Iliad*, namely, the problem of the individual hero, isolated by his own greatness and aspiration to the status of divinity, versus his need to remain a member of humanity so that his greatness may maintain relevance and understanding.

Patroclus responds to Nestor's statement of the claims of humanity and hurries off to Achilles, but on the way he is met by a wounded comrade, Eurypylus, limping out of the war with an arrow in his thigh. Eurypylus begs surgical aid from Patroclus, who knows the art of healing, since Machaon, the doctor, is himself hurt, and unable to help (we now know why Homer "planted" the wounding of Machaon). Patroclus wavers a moment, then decides that Achilles can wait; he chooses the act of mercy and stays to help Eurypylus. All this is quite in keeping with Patroclus's humane character. But the context is larger than the mere psychological constitution of Patroclus, and Homer invokes that larger context by including a seemingly unnecessary detail: he tells us just where Patroclus and

Eurypylus meet. They meet by the ship of Odysseus, where, he says, "there stood the council place, the judgment-seat, and the altars of the gods." Council, justice, religious observance—all of them are emblems of pious, civilized behavior of man toward man and of men toward the gods. One could fairly call them symbols of civilization itself, and Patroclus's help to his disabled friend takes its place in the ambience of the community of men, the community Achilles has rejected and no longer shares. By the use of an apparent irrelevancy, Homer has compelled this moment of his narrative to refract the heart of his poem. We can even see that it was in his mind to do so right from the start of Book 11, where, again for no obvious or necessary reason, he tells us where the ship of Odysseus was drawn up—at the mid-point of the Greek camp on the beachhead, a convenient place for calling aloud to either end of the camp.

But such procedure through associated image clusters may not only bring about amplification of significant moments in the narrative; it may also be closely connected with the very structure of the narrative and the kneading together of its tra-ditional parts. Perhaps the most striking example presents itself at the end of Book 2 and the beginning of Book 3. At the end of Book 2, Agamemnon, deceived by Zeus into expecting a final victory, marches his men out into the field with a great fanfare of similes and the long catalogue describing the various armed contingents. One expects that the next event will be a battle in which the Greeks will be defeated and the plan of Zeus to honor Achilles will begin to take effect. Quite the opposite happens. A truce is called by Hector, and it is decided to let Paris and Menelaus, Helen's two husbands (so to speak), fight it out in single combat and thus end the war without general bloodshed. Surely someone might have thought of that before! No less implausible is it, some lines later, to see Helen sitting with the Trojan elders on the wall, pointing out and identifying the leaders of the Achaean host, apparently for the first time, after a nine-year siege! We are even told that two of them, Odysseus and Menelaus, have already been in Troy on a diplomatic mission. Clearly, as many scholars have recognized, the poet has shifted his point of reference in time, quite without warning, and is now narrating events that properly belong to the first year of the war. This is true not only of Book 3, but also of the four books that follow it, for in the whole series of Books 3 to 7, Zeus's plan to honor Achilles is suspended. Nothing that happens affects the rest of the action in the least, and much that happens, including the fortification of the Greek camp (told in Book 7), must have been done shortly after the Greeks' arrival at Troy.

Yet these books must not be considered an interpolation, as they sometimes have been; it wants a visionary poet, not an interpolator, to contrive so bold a device as to put a five-book digression on the remote past between the preparations for a battle and the actual fighting. Homer had something in mind, which was no less than to include, however allusively, some account of the whole Trojan War, from its origins to its ninth year, within his chosen design of the single episode, Achilles' anger. But now that we have seen why he made this sudden shift, let us also observe how he made it; for it comes not altogether without warning. In Book 2, when Odysseus is persuading the disaffected army to remain and finish the war, he recalls to them a favorable portent that took place in Aulis, in Boeotia, where the host first mustered before sailing for Troy. This portent foretold victory in the tenth year of the war, but took place in the first. The next main episode after it that Homer narrates is the Catalogue of Ships, which, as most scholars agree, is based on another, separate poem describing the assembly of the Achaeans in Aulis, the rallying point for the attack. The poet's mind, and the minds of his audience, are transported for the nonce to that early point in the story. From that point the transition is easy to the events that immediately followed the Greeks' arrival in the Troad, like the death of Protesilaus (2. 700–702). Aulis, nowhere else mentioned in the

Iliad, serves as a kind of modulation, to use A. B. Lord's term, from one time to the other, and before we know it, we are back in the first year of the war. Homer might have used a flashback, as he did in the *Odyssey*—perhaps another reminiscence by Nestor—but such a leisurely device would not suit the intensity and drive of the *Iliad*. Instead, he ignored time altogether.

But the plan to include pictures of the whole war called for some account of the future as well. Homer supplies it, again in a succession of five books (18–22) narrating Achilles' exploits in revenge for Patroclus. No *tour de force* was necessary here, for it was well established in the minds of all that Hector's death meant the fall of the city, and the poet needed only to develop the symbolism of fire, closely associated with Achilles, to ornament his lines with images of cities captured and burning, and to sing the Battle of the Gods, where the gods who favor the Greeks overcome the protecting deities of Troy. The future, including the death of Achilles, is narrated by symbolic foreshadowings in an ever-deepening atmosphere of tragedy. But what of the present? The main story, of course, takes place in the present, but there is also its larger aspect, the impact of Achilles' angry retirement on the armies of both sides, the immediate effect of the Wrath. Homer takes account of this impact in yet a third series of five books describing the long, grim battle that fills the center of the *Iliad* (Books 11–15). Homer's total scheme thus emerges in all its shapeliness and abundance: at the core is the central drama of Achilles' wrath, told in four installments of two books each—Exposition (1 and 2), Complications (8 and 9), Reversal (16 and 17), Resolution (23 and 24)—spaced apart by three groups of five books each, with their respective vistas of past (3–7), present (11–15), and future (18–22). By virtue of his individual power of associating traditional themes through combined instincts for drama and symmetry, Homer has shaped his poem into what Keats said an epic should be: "Round, vast, and spanning all, like Saturn's ring."

But sometimes it happens that the poet's power of thematic

association can lead him to do things that are puzzling to the modern reader, though they were probably not so for Homer's ancient audiences, who, like the poet, knew the tradition well and could move about in it easily without getting confused, even when inconsistencies seemed to arise.

There are, for instance, some apparent contradictions in the behavior of Poseidon on a number of occasions in the *Iliad*. We may first take his attitude toward the Greek wall, built at the end of Book 7, *vis-à-vis* his feelings about the walls of Troy, built by himself and Apollo. Homer is interested in the Achaean wall and begins Book 12 with an extended, beautiful, but apparently irrelevant account of what happened to it. We are told how, after the city had fallen and the Achaeans had departed for home, Apollo diverted the eight rivers of the Troad against the wall, while Poseidon pried loose its foundations, with the result that the wall was totally demolished and its remains buried in the sand. Though the passage contributes nothing to the immediate action of the book, it is strangely haunting; also it provides a good example of how a traditional poet works by association of themes. Since the whole book is devoted to the Trojan attack on the Achaean wall and ends with Hector's breaking of its gate, it was natural for this partial, human destruction of the Greek wall to suggest its complete and final destruction by the gods. Thus the theme of "wall destruction" begins and ends the book, a kind of framing technique characteristically Homeric. So too it is regular for Homer, before entering upon the narrative of a human action, to give a gods'-eye view of it, and then gradually to narrow his focus on individual details. Thus he provides a long perspective on the action, and in this case the gods' concern with the wall, though a hostile one, enlarges that perspective.

But if we ask after the reason for this hostility, we find Poseidon's attitude somewhat at odds with itself. We are told twice that the Achaeans, when they built the wall, failed to make the requisite sacrifices to the gods. Now it was believed in antiquity that without sacrifice, sometimes human sacrifice, no structure could last. The failure to offer hecatombs, therefore, should have been enough to ensure the destruction of the wall. But we are told also that Poseidon was jealous of the wall, because its fame might cause future generations to forget the walls of Troy, which he and Apollo built. Yet in the *Iliad* Poseidon favors the Greeks and does everything he can to aid them in their attempt to take Troy and destroy its walls. Presumably, one reason, perhaps the chief reason, Poseidon supports the Greeks is that, after the walls of Troy had been built, Laomedon, father of Priam and a proverbial crook, had cheated him, and Apollo too, of the wages agreed upon, whereat Poseidon had sent a sea monster to ravage the coast. (Homer does not actually narrate the story of the cheat, but he knows of it, for he alludes to it very clearly in Book 20, 144ff.) There is, however, a manifest contradiction in Poseidon's attitude, which cannot be explained away. Poseidon hates Troy, but is very tender about its walls. Clearly, two traditions have met and only partly blended. The poet knew them both and used them at will, without undue scruples over literal consistency and logic. Here, partly by reason of the associations of the theme of wall destruction, and partly because he wanted to amplify it, he was led to insert the tale of what Poseidon and Apollo did when the war was over, and in so doing he touched, perhaps even accidentally, on another, different part of the great tradition.

Another, more glaring ambiguity in Poseidon's attitude comes in Book 20, when Achilles has returned to the war and is driving the Trojans before him. Apollo prompts Aeneas to make a stand against Achilles, and Poseidon, taking note of Apollo's action, proposes to Hera that they rescue Aeneas from certain death. Both Poseidon and Hera are, of course, anti-Trojan deities, and Hera refuses; but Poseidon goes alone and transports Aeneas, wrapped in a mist, to safety. This is the only time when a god who favors one side saves a hero on the other, and it comes as a surprise. Poseidon rationalizes his action, indeed, by pleading the fact that Aeneas is a pious, innocent man who is destined to rule over the surviving Trojans in time to come, so that the surprise is somewhat diminished; but the anomaly is there.

Aeneas is a somewhat strange figure in the *Iliad*, a bit remote and shadowy, not quite a part of the war. He accomplishes little, and speaks little except for the long harangue to Achilles about his ancestry. Three times he gets into mortal danger, and is rescued, once by his mother in Book 5, once in times past by Zeus (20. 194), and now by Poseidon (20. 290–352). His chief role seems to be to survive, to play the part of the "continuing" figure, associated with both past and future generations, so he must be rescued. But why by Poseidon? Either Aphrodite or Apollo might be his natural savior, but it was Apollo who urged him into this desperate strait. The whole situation is an inversion of what one would expect.

What seems to have happened is that Homer has shifted traditions and momentarily modulated into the story of Aeneas's adventures after the fall of Troy, when Poseidon, as we know from the *Aeneid*, became his protector. Or possibly he modulated into a version of the Trojan War in which Poseidon favors the Trojans. That there *was* such a tradition is all but proved by the opening lines of Euripides' *Trojan Women* (Poseidon is talking):

> For ever since upon this Trojan soil
> Phoebus and I, with rule and line, built up
> This girth of stone towers, never from my heart
> Has love for the city of my Trojans failed.
> [4–7]

There have been attempts to explain away, or edit out, this clear and explicit statement, but this other tradition, if Virgil is any witness, must have existed. Legends, it is well known, are committed to no single shape, but are subject to innumerable

variations that often become tangled. Poseidon's rescue of
Aeneas represents such a shift of traditions, and we may even
guess why Homer made it. In the early part of Book 20, before
the scene with Aeneas, the two opposing divine factions ranged
themselves against one another, each god with a specific antagonist. Poseidon's antagonist was Apollo, and it just might be
that the thematic opposition "Poseidon versus Apollo" operated
in the poet's mind to bring Poseidon into action, in answer to
Apollo's prompting of Aeneas to fight Achilles. But to do that he
needed a version in which Poseidon is well disposed toward
Aeneas, and accordingly he borrowed from it.

Thematic association, sometimes involving the conflation of
stories, is basic to Homer's poetic method. Books 20 and 21,
taken together, offer a magnificent example of the conflation of
two kinds of traditional tale, a battle of the gods, found in all
mythologies, and the common folktale of a hero's fight with a
river-god. Here the blending of the two stories produces, out of
primitive materials, what can only be called highly sophisticated
symbolism. It would have been easy simply to have the gods of
the Greek side overcome the gods of the Trojans, thus indicat-
ing that in the end the Achaeans did take Troy. But instead,
Homer has interrupted the theomachy and inserted Achilles'
struggle with, and victory over, the river Scamander (Xanthus),
the divine, tutelary stream of Troy. It is Achilles' desperate, and
almost fatal, efforts that are emphasized as the real force that, as
Pindar says, "cut the sinews of Ilium." His human struggle is
exalted, in all its tragic fierceness, by association with the divine
struggle, but also by contrast with it; for conversely, the actual
battle of the gods, when it finally takes place in Book 20, is
reduced to a comic brawl, at which Zeus laughs as Artemis sits
on his lap, weeping and complaining over the whipping that
Hera had just given her. The surrender of the river-god before
the flames of Hephaestus is the real foretoken of the city's fall.

Another example of the blending of two stories, again involving a degree of comedy, is the so-called deception of Zeus in

Book 14. Apparently part of a very ancient theological tradition, if it may be so called, was the "binding" of, or attempt to bind, a deity, either by deception or force. In Book 1, for instance, we hear of an attempt by Hera, Poseidon, and Athena to bind Zeus; in Book 14, we hear of how the god of Sleep, Hypnos, once put Zeus into deep slumber so that Hera could torment Heracles, in return for which Zeus suspended Hera by the wrists with anvils tied to her feet—a gentle admonition. The theme "binding a deity" could take many forms, and here again it is Sleep who is chosen as the means of rendering Zeus helpless after Hera has seduced him so that Poseidon may aid the Greeks. This "binding" reflects an ancient cosmogonic myth. Here it is joined to another very ancient story, also a ritual, a fertility rite known as the Sacred Marriage. Celebrated in various ways in various parts of Greece, the Sacred Marriage probably had its origins in the universal myth of the marriage of Heaven and Earth. Zeus is, of course, the immemorial sky-god of the Indo-Europeans, and Hera was probably, in origin, an earth-goddess.[4] By combining this beautiful and solemn myth with the binding of Zeus, Homer has turned it into an episode of deception, seduction, and at least threatened retaliation. Motifs from the Sacred Marriage appear, such as Hera's ritual bath and the flowers that spring up as the union is consummated, but Hera has anything but fertility in mind. Neither has Zeus; he lists with relish a generous selection of his former mistresses, by way of assuring his wife that, for the moment, she is more fascinating than any of them. (Unpleasant as she is, we are reminded that Hera, too, has had some things to put up with.) Then they make love, Zeus sleeps, and we return to the battlefield, where Poseidon is now free to help the Achaeans openly. The whole scene is high comedy, as Homer tells it; but it is compounded of two very serious myths.

4.   [See Whitman, "Hera's Anvils," *Harvard Studies in Classical Philology* 74 (1970):37–42, for the underlying cosmogonic myth and Hera's role as an ancient goddess of earth.]

Actually, there is probably a little more to the deception of Zeus than is contained in Book 14. As it is told there, Hera is acting quite on her own, as is Poseidon in helping the Greeks. But the likelihood is that they conspired together. Much earlier, in Book 8 (198ff.), there is a brief and apparently pointless conversation between the two on Olympus. Zeus's plan to defeat the Greeks in honor of Achilles is just beginning to take effect, and Hera turns in anger to Poseidon with the proposal that they could, by cooperating, successfully oppose Zeus. Poseidon replies that they could not, and there the matter is dropped, leaving the reader wondering why the scene is there at all. But, though Poseidon has denied that they could oppose Zeus, the next we hear of him he is in Samothrace waiting for a chance to do just that. What seems to have happened is a case of the poet's thinking forward, as Zeus's plan to honor Achilles begins, to what Hera and Poseidon did about the defeat of the Greeks which that plan entails. Homer begins to narrate a traditional conspiracy between them, but, not being ready to tell the whole story, he hints at it, breaks off, and continues the brief battle of Book 8. By the time he resumes this episode, he has neglected to tell us what changed Poseidon's mind or how he got to Samothrace. The details of the conspiracy are left untold, but that there was one seems clear from the brief speech of Hypnos in Book 14:

Now, Poseidon, help the Greeks to your heart's content,
And grant them glory, though but for a little, while Zeus still sleeps;
For I have wrapped a gentle stupor round him,
And Hera deceived him into lying in the bed of love.

[357ff.]

Hypnos's speech has the ring of one who is reporting the success of a concerted plan. Clearly, Poseidon had been persuaded to help the Greeks by Hera's plan to put Zeus to sleep, but instead of telling us so, the poet sings separately of Poseidon on the battlefield and Hera with Zeus on Mount Ida.[5]

Such confusions between two or more ways of telling a tale, with consequent omissions and inconsistencies, are common in oral traditions; a notorious Homeric example occurs in the *Odyssey*, where the plans of Odysseus and Telemachus for killing the suitors differ greatly as laid down in Book 16 and as carried out in 19. An even more interesting, and quite parallel, example of omission of a necessary detail can be found in one version of the Yugoslav epic of Marko and Nina. Parry collected four versions of this song, which tells of the celebrated hero Marko Kraljević, who is summoned by the sultan to serve in the army for a certain length of time (the length varies from version to version).[6] When Marko presents himself, the sultan takes away his horse and his sword, presumably to transform him from a border-fighter into a regular soldier. In Marko's absence, his enemy Nina (a man's name) mistreats his family, and Marko begs for a furlough in which to get revenge. The sultan accedes, returns the horse and the sword, and Marko goes and kills Nina. That is the bare outline in three of the versions; but in a fourth the singer forgets to tell us that the sultan took away Marko's horse and sword, though he does tell us that he returned them; if we had only that version we would be rather mystified.

Now such an omission is a defect, of course, a defect we would like to think Homer incapable of. But it must also be said that in the telling of traditional stories an omission of this sort is less of a defect than it would be in, say, a modern short story,

5. [The details of this interpretation of the interaction of Hera and Poseidon in *Iliad* 14 are worked out in Whitman's forthcoming article, "Sequence and Simultaneity in *Iliad* N, Ξ, O," *Harvard Studies in Classical Philology* 85 (1981): 1–15 (with Ruth Scodel).]

6. [The Yugoslav song "Marko and Nina" is discussed, with translations of some of the versions, by A. B. Lord, *The Singer of Tales*, Harvard Studies in Comparative Literature 24 (Cambridge, Mass., 1960), pp. 71–75, 113–17, 236–41.]

because the listening audience knows the tradition and can easily supply the missing information, so that the loss is not greatly felt. The same principle of presuming upon one's audience's knowledge is at work in certain passages of the *Iliad*, where the poet's style becomes so allusive in narrating some episode in the past, that it is almost impossible for us to understand fully what is happening. Glaucus's story of Bellerophon in Book 6 is the most notable of these, but there are others, too. The traditional poet did not have to spell everything out.

All these examples involve comparatively minor episodes. But even the main theme of the *Iliad* is an example of the modulation, or blending, of two separate kinds of traditional story. The retirement from war of a hero whose honor has somehow been damaged is a fairly common theme found in many heroic tales throughout many unrelated cultures. It seems to be part of a hero's career for him to get angry and sulk at some point; in Persian epic, it is the great Rustam; in Arthurian legend, it is Sir Lancelot, though from a somewhat different cause. In the *Iliad* there are several sulking heroes besides Achilles himself. Paris, in Book 6, after being defeated by Menelaus, is found lurking in his bedchamber, and is rebuked by Hector for sulking instead of fighting. Aeneas, too, in Book 13, hangs back behind the lines in a kind of semiretirement, angry because he felt that Priam did not honor him properly. The most striking example, of course, is Meleager, whose story is told in Book 9 by Phoenix to Achilles, as a warning against refusing Agamemnon's reparations and rejecting the Embassy. Through the oral poet's traditional means of expansion and diminution, the theme "heroic sulk" could be treated in a passing remark (Aeneas), a short scene (Paris and Meleager), or as the plot of a 15,000-line epic. Its normal pattern is (a) the hero's retirement, (b) his rejection of repeated offers and appeals to return, and (c) his return when the situation gets desperate enough, with or without having accepted the offered amends.

A complete version may be found in another Yugoslavian

poem about the hero Marko Kraljević, who is fighting for the
sultan and presenting him daily with multitudes of the enemy's
heads. In jealousy at his exploits, his enemies accuse him to the
sultan of presenting heads cut off by others. Marko retires to his
tent in a rage, rejects a whole series of appeals to return, declar-
ing that he will return "only when the enemy reaches the sultan's tent." They do, and he then returns and slaughters them.
(One might almost suspect that the author of that song had been
reading the *Iliad*.) The resemblance to the stand taken by Achilles is striking; his final decision too, in Book 9, is that he will
fight only when the battle reaches his own tent and ships.

But there is a slight difference. Marko Kraljević rejects many
embassies, Achilles only one. Homer seems not to be quite
completing the pattern. Yet there is a passage in Book 11 which
indicates that he easily might have; at lines 609–610 Achilles
says to Patroclus:

> Now, I expect, the Achaeans will stand about my knees
> In supplication, for unbearable need is coming upon them.

Of course, in Book 9, just the preceding night, the Achaeans
have done exactly that, so that Denys Page and many others
have felt that these two lines are inconsistent with the Embassy
and could have been written only by another poet who knew
nothing of Agamemnon's first offer and appeal.[7] But not at all.
Homer knew the rules for this kind of story, and so, of course,
did Achilles. Achilles fully expects more appeals to come, and
he fully expects to refuse them, for that is the traditional pattern
of the retiring hero. An angry hero is not easily appeased. Achilles, of course, expects also to yield eventually, and on the terms
that he laid down. What he does not foresee is that he will
return to battle under far different, far more bitter circumstances
than are called for by the story he thinks he is living out.

7. Denys Page, *History and the Homeric Iliad*, Sather Classical Lectures 31
(Berkeley and Los Angeles, 1959), pp. 305–307.

For, in the end, Homer does not complete the pattern of the hero retired in anger; he modulates into a different, equally traditional theme, one in which there is no high-hearted victory over jealous enemies or unappreciative friends. Before the battle reaches Achilles' ships, the point at which he said that he would fight, Patroclus is slain in armor borrowed from him while trying to stem the defeat of the Greeks, and at this juncture begins a new story, one that centers around the frequent heroic theme of revenge for a slain comrade. Throughout the *Iliad*, warriors, at seeing a fellow soldier fall, rush forward, filled with rage and grief, to take vengeance. It is part of the deathly rhythm of war, and often it costs the avenger his life, too.

In the case of Achilles, Homer had such a story ready-made. According to another tradition, Achilles' greatest friend was not Patroclus, but Nestor's son Antilochus, who died in the effort to save his father's life on the battlefield; he succeeded, but was slain by Memnon, the Ethiopian prince who had joined the Trojan cause. Achilles was warned by his mother not to avenge Antilochus, for if he did, his own death would soon follow. In the lost epic *Aithiopis,* by Arctinus of Miletus, it was told how Achilles nonetheless avenged Antilochus by slaying Memnon, and was then killed under the walls of Troy by the arrow of Paris, directed by Apollo. No doubt Homer, who may possibly have been the teacher of Arctinus, was able to sing this song; he certainly knew the story. But in the *Iliad* he did not relate the death of Achilles or go into the story of Memnon and Antilochus at all. He did, however, wish to dramatize the shortness of Achilles' life and the hero's own deliberate sacrifice of it in the act of avenging a friend.

What he seems to have done, therefore, is to borrow from the Antilochus story and expropriate from it the prophecy that Achilles would fall if he avenged such and such a comrade, substituting Patroclus for Antilochus (cf. 18. 88–106). Often in traditions involving many heroic figures, the same episode is told about several, and Homer may not have been the only bard to make Achilles' death dependent on vengeance for Patroclus, rather than for Antilochus; one can even imagine bards vigorously disputing the matter. The point is that Homer in the *Iliad* makes his central narrative thread out of two different strands of tradition, two quite distinct genres in the repertoire of heroic fiction—the tale of the offended hero, which he leaves incomplete, and the tale of revenge for a fallen friend. The first unified tragic plot in Greek or Western literature is the product of the familiar bardic practice of the modulation of traditional themes.

The theme of Achilles' early death is so crucial to the *Iliad* that we must look at two other passages where it enters, indirectly, as it must in a poem not designed to include it as part of the narrative. The first passage, which has always puzzled scholars, again offers an example of the poet's modulating within the tradition, or better, traditions, for at this point Homer seems almost to have been derailed into the story of Achilles' death under the walls of Troy, after slaying Memnon in revenge for Antilochus. In Book 22, just after killing Hector, Achilles turns to the Achaeans and says:

> O friends, leaders and marshals of the Argives,
> Since the gods have granted me to subdue this man
> Who did us much harm, more than all the rest,
> Come, let us make trial in arms around the city,
> That we may learn of what mind the Trojans are,
> Whether, now he is fallen, they will abandon their lofty city,
> Or stoutly hold out, though Hector no longer lives.
> But why does my heart speak to me so?
> There by the ships, unwept, unburied lies
> Patroclus, and I shall not forget him while I live
> Among the living, and while my knees uphold me.
>
> [22. 378–88]

He proceeds to countermand his order to attack and proposes to return to conduct Patroclus's funeral. This speech contains a strange, apparently ill-motivated reversal of purpose. In the moment of supreme victory it is only natural for Achilles to urge a general, final assault on the city itself, as he seems about to do here (381–84). But suddenly Achilles changes his mind: Patroclus must have his obsequies first; the war can wait. This too is natural if one remembers that right at the outset in Book 1 Achilles said that he had nothing against the Trojans; he killed Hector only in revenge for Patroclus, whose burial might well take precedence with him over the completion of Agamemnon's cause.

Why then does Homer have him think at all about taking the city? Achilles' change of mind is surprising, not to say a bit jolting, and scholars have not been slow in finding here the clumsy hand of some redactor of the poem. But the true answer should now be clear; it lies in this realm of association we have been discussing, and there has been no mistake or failure on the poet's part. Homer did not intend to narrate the death of Achilles, but neither did he intend his audience to forget it and simply concentrate on the victory over Hector. Perhaps we should say that Homer himself could not forget it, for he was about to close his poem with the incomparable episode of Priam and Achilles in Book 24, in which Achilles' consciousness of his own impending doom is the tragic force that enables him to accept Priam, give back the body of Hector, and recover his own humanity. Achilles' self-chosen death must be kept in mind, so that when he proposes an immediate attempt on the city, only to reject the idea, we may see a momentary modulation, through association of themes, into the version that told of Achilles' death under the walls. After seven lines, the poet has Achilles recover himself with the formulaic line, "But why does my heart speak so to me?"—a line the Homeric hero always uses in debating two alternatives with himself and rejecting one. Should we say that where two traditions are so similar in plot a singer might well slip mistakenly from one into the other? That might be the answer, or part of it. But it is far more

likely that Homer deliberately wanted to recall the circumstances of Achilles' death and therefore quite knowingly borrowed from the Antilochus-Memnon story, where Achilles'
death follows upon his decision to avenge that other companion, Antilochus. Most likely he is combining the two stories and
making an almost automatic shift by association on the theme
"Achilles' death," which has almost obsessively haunted the
poet's mind since the beginning of Book 18 when Thetis
foretells it and Achilles chooses it. We are reminded of it again
by the prophecy of Achilles' horse at the end of 19, by Achilles
himself as he slays Lycaon in 21, and also by the dying Hector.
We are always reminded that Achilles is taking vengeance on
himself as well as on Hector.

Perhaps the most vivid reminder comes just as Achilles is
about to drive his spear into Hector's body, as the duel in Book
22 approaches its catastrophe. Hector is wearing Achilles' armor, stripped from the body of Patroclus. He put it on in Book
17, when rebuked by Glaucus for not fighting hard enough,
without doubt because he felt that in so doing he was putting on
heightened valor and strength, even as Patroclus did when he
borrowed these arms from Achilles. In the *Iliad*, it must be
remembered, there is a very close association between a hero
and his arms, an association that amounts almost to identification, and certainly involves a kind of primitive, fixed symbolism, whose meaning sometimes takes precedence over reason and logic. For example, men may exchange armor in the
heat of battle when there is no time to do so, or a hero is said to
put on his arms when he is already wearing them—meaning
simply that he girded himself with valor.

This symbolism of armor has been often recognized, but in
the duel between Hector and Achilles, it becomes the vehicle
for the central tragedy of the poem. In most duels in the *Iliad*,
the point of view is evenly divided between the two contestants;
but almost the whole of Book 22 is narrated from Hector's point
of view: we hear his dilemma in the great soliloquy, we see the

approaching Achilles through his eyes, and in the simile of the
nightmare of fleeing and pursuit, it is Hector's nightmare, not
Achilles'. It is Hector who is cruelly deceived by Athena and at
last recognizes that death is upon him. But just before the fatal
thrust (321ff.), the point of view shifts, and we see through the
eyes of Achilles. Achilles is looking for a chink in Hector's
armor, and the poet is careful to tell us that it is the armor
stripped from Patroclus, Achilles' own. Arms *are* the man, or at
least the warrior, and the dramatic, sudden change in point of
view underscores Achilles' determination to destroy himself.
The death of Hector and that of Achilles are both accomplished, the one in fact, the other symbolically, by a single
stroke of the Pelean spear.

Somehow, when Homer presents us with such moments, we
never think to pity him for being unable to write. Like Rudyard
Kipling's caveman, "He couldn't read and he couldn't write,
and he didn't want to." We might add, "and he didn't have to."
For however the epics may have gotten first recorded—which is
another long, controversial story—Homer's poems bear on
every page the tokens of oral composition within a traditional
verse medium reaching back for centuries into the unexplorable
dimness of the Indo-European past.

The art of Homer demands wondering admiration, not tol-
erant patronage, and we need not somehow contrive to thrust a
pen upon him. Oral composition may have its hazards, but it
also has its advantages. The poet's mind, working at the high
speed required by formulaic verse-making, must rely on instant
association of themes and images, for association is a far more
rapid mode of cognition than is any rational process. Not sur-
prisingly, therefore, it seems that the association of themes, or
stories, is fully as accountable for the planning of certain parts of
the poem as the poet is, that is, the poet's conscious intent.
Such associations may lead to a digression, a slight dislocation
in the narrative, or merely to an added touch, seemingly
perhaps irrelevant, but suggestive of larger meanings.

In Book 14, for example, Homer suddenly, and apparently for no reason, inserts into a spirited battle-narrative the line: "And the sea crashed along the tents and ships of the Argives" (14. 392). What the sea was doing at such a tense moment might seem beside the point. But Poseidon is now openly helping the Greeks and has been mentioned in the lines immediately preceding. Poseidon is, in a way, the sea, and the mention of his name prompts mention of his domain. The line adds an elemental touch to the description of the battle, and leads on, in its turn, to a massive sea-simile.

It is the rich, measureless tradition that makes all this possible. Not only is the formulaic language traditional; the story patterns, themes, and motifs all come from a bardic heritage that it was the individual singer's task to master to the full and exploit in the interest of his poetic intention. It is possible that Homer added some elements of his own—new formulas, similes of his own devising, or whatever—but if he did so, he made them on the analogy of existing elements, and no attempt to isolate them can achieve any certainty. Selection, arrangement, amplification, and diminution constitute the oral poet's technique for making a traditional poem his own. We have seen how much of Homer's poetic art lies in his controlled use of themes, motifs, and kinds of story, and how, by association, modulation, and awareness of symbolic values he constructs his meaning. One might go on at greater length, or take many a different approach, but the conclusion would, I think, be the same: that the *Iliad* is at once traditional, and uniquely Homer's creation.

4. Some Anomalies in the *Iliad* and the Problem of Oral Transmission

In Book 7 of the *Iliad*, after the interrupted duel of Ajax and Hector, Nestor makes some proposals that have bothered critics from Aristarchus on. Though the Greeks have been far from defeated in the day's action, Nestor speaks as if they had been and suggests a truce, a gathering of the dead, and the building of a wall to protect the ships (7. 327–43). The critics object that if the Achaeans were to fortify their camp, they would have done so immediately upon landing and could not have survived for nine years on an undefended beachhead.[1] This reasoning is perfectly logical. But, as I've tried to show in the preceding chapter, all the events in Books 3 to 7 would be more fitting for the first year of the war, or at least its earlier years, the Teichoscopia and duel in Book 3 being, of course, the most obvious ones.[2]

If Homer had wanted, as I believe, to include in his poem not merely the main dramatic narrative but also, by indirection, some account of the Trojan war tradition as a whole, he had his choice of two ways of doing it, either by a formal flashback, such as the *Odyssey* contains, or by ignoring chronological

1. Thuc. 1. 11. 1; see Denys Page, *History and the Homeric Iliad*, Sather Classical Lectures 31 (Berkeley and Los Angeles, 1959), pp. 315–24; G. S. Kirk, *The Songs of Homer* (Cambridge, 1962), p. 229.

2. Whitman, *Homer and the Heroic Tradition* (Cambridge, Mass., 1958), pp. 265–70.

sequence altogether and narrating long-past events as if they were just then occurring. He chose the latter, and the wall is no more anomalous than the Teichoscopia. Moreover, having it built before our eyes makes it more natural for him to introduce the theme of Poseidon's jealousy, which in turn leads to the superb opening of Book 12, where, by a flash-forward, it is told how Poseidon and Apollo in later years destroyed the wall and buried it under the sands of the Hellespont,[3] a fine perspective, somewhat akin to the *Odyssey*'s retrospective gaze at the war in Troy.

But the wall is not Nestor's only misdeed in this passage. He proposes also that they gather the dead, burn them "a little apart from the ships, so that each man may bring bones home to the children, whenever we set sail for our homeland," and then build an abundant tumulus over the pyre. *Locus conclamatus; damnavit Aristarchus.* How would it be possible for the individual bones to be taken back if they were buried in a common tomb? Leaf remarks also that the phrase ὥς κ᾽ ὀστέα παισὶν ἕκαστος / οἴκαδ᾽ ἄγῃ should properly mean, "so that each man may bring back his own bones to his children" (7. 334f.).[4] (It *could* be so translated.) But worst of all, taking bones home from a war is not found elsewhere in Homer, and Jacoby has demonstrated, much to the delight of Denys Page, that such a practice was unknown anywhere in Greece until 464 B.C., when a law providing for such transportation was passed at Athens.[5] The logical conclusion is, then, that these lines were inserted into the *Iliad* after 464—by an idiot, with no adequate knowledge of the mortician's art. And yet Jacoby's date provides only negative evidence, at best an argument from silence. One cannot prove that before 464 no bones had ever been brought back from a war

3. Cf. *Il.* 14. 31–32, where it is practically stated that the wall was built in the first year; but see Walter Leaf, ed., *The Iliad*, 2d ed. (London, 1900–1902), ad 14. 31 (end of note).

4. Leaf, ad *Il.* 7. 334–35.

5. Page, p. 323; F. Jacoby, "Patrios Nomos," *Journal of Hellenic Studies* 64 (1944):37ff.; Kirk, p. 180.

or that somewhere along the line the epic tradition had not picked up knowledge of the custom. In fact, if one wanted to be strictly logical, one would have to say that 464 is the first we hear of bringing home bones, *except* for this passage in the *Iliad*. (We may add that at 16. 454–457 Zeus orders Sleep and Death to return Sarpedon's body to Lycia for burial, although bones are not mentioned).

As for the inconsistency in the burial mode, is it really so glaring? If we look at what happens in Book 23, at the funeral of Patroclus, the issue becomes a little more understandable. There, in a highly elaborated development of a funeral scene, the poet makes Achilles give instructions as follows:

Then let us gather the bones of Patroclus,
Carefully distinguishing them; they are quite conspicuous,
For they lie in the middle of the pyre; the others
Were burned in a jumble around the edges, horses and men.
And let us put them in a golden vessel . . .
Until I descend into Hades;
And I bid you make a mound, but a small one. . . .
Later, you will make a broad, high one for me.

[238–47]

In this vivid and detailed passage, we may notice two or three motifs that make up the full funeral theme: burning, distinguishing and gathering of bones, urn burial, and provision for subsequent disposal;[6] nothing, indeed, about taking bones home—that remains unique (except for Sarpedon); but in other respects the parallels are clear. The main difference between this scene and the earlier one is that here the singer, on a highly important occasion, has developed the theme in detail, while in Nestor's speech he produced it in briefer compass, omitting the

6. Note that Patroclus's bones, covered with fat and put into the "golden vessel" (*Il.* 23, 243), are not placed under the tumulus Achilles orders to be built (23. 245), but are stored in the tent (23. 253f.; see also Leaf ad 254). [See also Emily Vermeule, *Aspects of Death in Early Greek Art and Poetry*, Sather Classical Lectures 46 (Berkeley and Los Angeles, 1979), pp. 59n.37, 226].

distinguishing and gathering of bones and any mention of urn burial. It is regular practice among oral poets to expand or contract themes at will, and unlike modern scholars, the ancient audience could be counted on to grasp what was happening without always having it spelled out.

Book 23 has another famous problem. In the Games, there is one contest nobody likes, the duel between Ajax and Diomedes. Achilles offers a panoply to the one who first "touches insides through armor and black blood" (ψαύσῃ δ᾽ ἐνδίνων διά τ᾽ ἔντεα καὶ μέλαν αἷμα [806]). Walter Leaf thought the whole scene monstrous, and G. S. Kirk finds it "as inept in expression as it is absurd in meaning."[7] Actually, to my taste, it is rather exciting to have the two best fighters after Achilles engage in a friendly but blood-drawing fencing match with spears. But the real trouble lies in line 806, the one quoted, specifically the word ἐνδίνων, which should, according to the scholiast, mean "entrails." "Reaching entrails" (rather than just drawing blood) does seem a little far for the two heroes to carry their sport; for that reason— and also because the rest of it was reputedly borrowed from Book 10—the line was judged spurious by some ancient commentators.

Of course, the line could be an insertion by someone who wanted to add a little extra excitement to the scene, however silly it might sound. On the other hand, ἔνδινα is a *hapax legomenon* and does not have to mean "entrails," for which the regular Homeric words are ἔντερα, ἔγκατα, or σπλάγχνα. All it has to mean is "What is inside something" and need not mean anything so deep as the liver or intestines.[8] Besides, brave

7. Leaf, ad *Il*. 13. 806; Kirk, pp. 205, 223.
8. Hesychius and other ancient interpreters take the phrase to mean "inside the armor." See also P. Chantraine, *Dictionnaire étymologique de la langue grecque*, s.v. ἔνδον, who calls ἔνδινα "un dérivé remarquable." [The second half of 23. 806 remains syntactically difficult. Possibly the phrase, like *Il*. 10. 298, is meant to evoke a picture of bloody armor, although not very much blood (unlike 10. 298) would be required. It is also possible that the formulaic analogy with a battle scene and lack of precise knowledge of this kind of fencing caused Homer to nod slightly. Another possibility is that ἐνδίνων arose from confusion with a present participle.]

men play dangerous games: medieval jousts were often fatal to
many of the combatants, and I have learned from Bernard Knox
that certain French officers during World War II amused themselves by standing in a circle and throwing, with a sudden back-
handed spin, a sharpened axe at one another, sending it each
time in as unexpected a direction as possible. The man to whom
it came was to catch it (it was hoped) by the handle. They played
this game without armor.

Another allegedly anomalous passage is in Book 17 (140–95),
in which Hector slips behind the lines to put on Achilles' armor, recently stripped from Patroclus. Hector had just been
rebuked by Glaucus for slacking; he excuses himself, and says
that he will show Glaucus a great deed of valor. But instead of
doing anything dashing, he retires, changes armor, and returns.
This is not, as Kirk calls it, a minor inconsequence;[9] it is an
exploitation of armor as the symbol of the heroic role. Armor
has something to do with the self, and when Patroclus wears this
same armor, he becomes unlike his usual self, gentle and unassuming, and very like Achilles. As Hector puts it on, he doubtless feels that he, too, will be somehow the greater for it. (Zeus,
looking on, however, shakes his head with disapproval, for Hector is not the man to wear that armor with success [17. 198–208].)
Scholars have wondered, couldn't Homer have chosen a more
tactful time for him to don it? In point of fact it is quite a tactful
time, for Hector puts on, or tries to put on, a greater self in
response to Glaucus's taunt. Nor is the episode unparalleled in
its disregard of plausibility in favor of symbolism. In Book 14
(370ff.), in a desperate moment of fighting, Diomedes and
Odysseus, at the prompting of Poseidon, make all the chieftains
change their armor, the best men putting on the best arms, the
lesser men the less distinguished. Unlikely as the maneuver may
be under such circumstances, from the practical point of view

9. Kirk, p. 221. The scholium on *Il.* 17. 186 objected too: see Leaf, *ad
loc.*

(and Agamemnon has just earlier been reproved by Odysseus for
an equally unlikely one), I feel less inclined to believe that the
passage was dreamed up by someone who had a grudge against
Homer, than to see it in the symbolic light I suggest. Finally, in
the case of Hector's change, it might be added that Homer has
plans for that armor. Hector will be wearing it when he confronts Achilles for what will be his last battle in Book 22. If one
is right in seeing armor as in some sense "self," as I suggested in
the previous chapter, Homer could scarcely have reminded us
more pointedly that Hector's death implies Achilles' own, and
that in this moment of slaying, two victims, not just one, fall by
a single thrust.

Some real anomalies do exist in the *Iliad*. I cannot explain,
for instance—and no one else has explained—the use of the
dual number in Book 9 (182ff.) for three envoys and two
heralds; or why Achilles in greeting his three visitors says "Hail
to you both" (9. 147). Probably the best explanation is, as Kirk
indeed recognizes, that there was a form of the Embassy in
which there were only two envoys, Ajax and Odysseus, and that
Phoenix was added in the version we have.[10] So there has been
a reworking, no doubt, but there is no more evidence for multiple authorship, in the sense intended by Kirk and Denys Page,
than there is for single. Homer himself, it seems more likely,
could have sung either a two-man Embassy poem or one with
three men and forgotten momentarily to change his duals to
plurals when he did the latter. It seems less likely that an interpolator would have neglected this detail. It remains incorrect
Greek, however, and the really surprising thing is that it was
never edited out. On the other hand, it is not unique: in at least
one other place in the *Iliad*, there is such an irrational dual,[11]

---

10. Kirk, p. 218; see also Page, p. 298. [The most recent discussion I have
seen, with updated bibliography, is R. Gordesiani, "Zur Interpretation der
Duale im 9. Buch der Ilias," *Philologus* 124 (1980):163–74. Discussion of the
problematical duals continues unabated].

11. *Iliad* 5. 487; see also 8. 73f. and Leaf ad loc.

and in the eighth book of the *Odyssey* the dual is used with fifty-two young men as subject.[12] Could Zenodotus have been right, that the dual could be used interchangeably with the plural? That seems hardly likely, but in three places Homer uses it, and there are no manuscript variants.

There are numerous other such oddities, of course, which may always remain unexplained. But in any case the theory of multiple authorship does little to help such a passage as stands in Book 19 (76ff.), where Agamemnon, "not standing up, but speaking from where he sat," says, "O friends, when a man stands up (to make a speech) it is good to listen and not interrupt." Here, however, there are ancient manuscript variants; the Massilian and Chiote texts say something quite different, and not at all self-contradictory,[13] so that the question is, really, on what authority did the creator of the vulgate choose the reading he did, and was he right?

On the other hand, there are alleged anomalies that simply do not exist. Denys Page has argued that the poet who wrote Achilles' big speech in the beginning of Book 16 had never heard of the Embassy in Book 9.[14] How could Achilles, after having been approached the evening before by the Embassy offering amends, still say, "The Trojans would have filled all the ditches with their corpses if only Agamemnon would be friendly toward me" (ἤπια εἰδείη) (16. 71–73)? This statement, Page argues, is inconsistent with the Embassy. But Achilles is not ignoring the Embassy; he is criticizing it. The phrase ἤπια εἰδείη, as I have argued elsewhere, means precisely what was lacking in Agamemnon's offer—true courtesy, affection, friendliness.[15]

---

12. *Od.* 8. 35–36, 48–49; 12. 52; 16.7. For discussion and bibliography on the anomalous duals see Page, p. 299n1, pp. 324–25. Page is skeptical of the broader use of the dual.

13. See Leaf, ad *Il.* 19. 76–77; also *Od.* 13. 56.

14. Page, pp. 307–12.

15. Whitman, *Homer*, p. 193n36.

Kirk, be it said, is skeptical of Page's argument,[16] but he need not have put his disagreement so mildly, for the refutation does not depend very much on the interpretation of ἤπια εἰδείη. One need only go back a dozen lines in this same speech: "But let bygones be bygones, one can't be angry forever; and yet indeed I said I would not quell my wrath until the war-cry and battle came to my own ships" (16. 60–63). Now there is only one place where Achilles said that, and it is in Book 9, lines 650ff., and the poet of 16 is building quite directly on 9. But, urges Page, Achilles warns Patroclus not to steal Achilles' own honor by distinguishing himself too much, so that the Achaeans may return the lovely girl to him and gifts besides. Such a statement contradicts Achilles' violent rejection of the girl and the gifts in Book 9.[17]

Part of the answer to this apparent contradiction is that sulking heroes traditionally reject many embassies, as we have seen from the Slavic parallels in the previous chapter. But also, characters in the epic often speak with the poet's knowledge, not just their own. They speak their total situation, one might say, and to have them do so serves various purposes—sometimes ironic, sometimes prophetic, sometimes simply informational for the audience's sake. The poet knows that Achilles will get Briseis back, plus gifts, even if Achilles does not; so that the proper way of looking at this remark is, Homer is anticipating Book 19, not ignoring Book 9.

The case is a bit different in Book 11 when Achilles sends Patroclus out to Nestor, as the defeat of the Greeks is beginning. He says: "Now, I ween, the Achaeans will stand about my knees beseeching, for unbearable need has assailed them" (11. 608–9). This remark, too, is supposed to show ignorance of the Embassy, where precisely such beseeching had taken place, but there is no need for such a conclusion. Achilles quite rea-

16. Kirk, p. 215.
17. Cf. *Il.* 9. 378ff. and 16. 83–87; see Leaf, ad 16. 85.

sonably expects further, and, he hopes, politer, overtures from the Greeks when they've been beaten badly enough; and he has stated the conditions on which he will help them—when his own ships are in danger.

But there are other places where a character speaks with the poet's knowledge rather than his own. One of the best examples is Hector's great speech to Andromache, in which he acknowledges the inevitable doom of Troy and imagines details of Andromache's enslavement to a Greek lord (*Iliad* 6. 447–65). How does Hector know all that? He can't really know it, but the poet knows it, and he lets Hector say it in order to achieve a tragic effect that has seldom been equaled. So too, in the eleventh book of the *Odyssey*, Agamemnon's shade, after rehearsing the tale of his own murder by Clytemnestra, tells Odysseus not to worry about Penelope's murdering Odysseus (11. 444–46). How can Agamemnon be so sure? The answer is he cannot, but Homer could, and he put the lines where he did to emphasize the contrast in wives.

If the answers I have tried to bring to these "anomalies" seem each a little ad hoc, so too are the anomalies themselves. Analytic scholarship has tended to overemphasize isolated individual details at the expense of the impact of the whole. Consider the end of the *Odyssey:* it is damned specifically on the grounds of language, style, structure, ignorance of either the road to Hades or the geography thereof, and generally for being otiose and anticlimactic. I would have liked to deal with this problem a little, but in any case W. B. Stanford has shown with such systematic rigor that the end of the *Odyssey* is ethically necessary, that the matter might almost stop there.[18] I hope to show sometime that the linguistic and stylistic anomalies are also mythical monsters, not real ones; but perhaps enough has

18. W. B. Stanford, "The Ending of the *Odyssey:* An Ethical Approach," *Hermathena* 100 (1965):5–20 and *The Ulysses Theme* (Oxford, 1954; repr. Ann Arbor, 1968), pp. 56–61. [For more recent discussion and bibliography, concluding in favor of Homeric authorship, see Dorothea Wender, *The Last Scenes of the Odyssey*, Mnemosyne Supplement 52 (Leiden, 1978)].

been said to indicate that the peculiarites in Homer, of whatever kind, do not of necessity point to multiple authorship, whether of the extreme kind envisioned by Denys Page or of the more prudent variety of Kirk. The incomprehension may be due to our ignorance, rather than to that of interpolators, reproducers, rhapsodes, and bad singers.

It is sometimes argued that the oral tradition "degenerated" or was infiltrated and sapped by the advance of literacy.[19] These terms are misleading. A. B. Lord says explicitly that it is not writing itself that kills an oral tradition, but the arrival of a fixed text that is looked upon as authoritative.[20] Until such a text appears, for whatever reason, good and bad singers coexist in the tradition producing songs according to their talents; the Slavic tradition could and did include an Avdo Međedović in a century when oral poetry is on the wane. The decline, hence, is quantitative rather than qualitative. Oral poetry died out in Greece we know not when, but perhaps very late in some places—in some, perhaps never. It became less and less popular, no doubt, as new literary forms developed and as the fixed text used by the rhapsodes became the authoritative Homer. But there is no reason to think it degenerated in quality, necessarily, or that there could have been no good singers in the sixth century. There must have been bad ones, too, and to one of these we may owe the *Shield of Heracles*, but in fact we cannot date that poem with certainty; it could be as old as Homer, or nearly. My point is that one need not invent a whole process of degeneration to account for parts of the epic one finds tasteless or obscure. Such judgments are the purest subjectivity, and tastes may differ. Some subsequent singers may possibly have done Homer damage (or perhaps good), but until we can see how their contributions were recorded and why, it is best to let them be.

Let me briefly say what I think happened. For some

19. Kirk, pp. 91–98.
20. A. B. Lord, *The Singer of Tales*, Harvard Studies in Comparative Literature 24 (Cambridge, Mass., 1960), pp. 129–38.

reason—either, as I once wrote, to accommodate the epics to
festival performance[21] or, as Lord suggests, because oriental
influence prompted the Greeks to become interested in record-
ing things[22]—Homer's poems were recorded by dictation to a
scribe by the poet himself. As Lord has convincingly argued,
Homer availed himself of the advantages of dictation in order to
compose "the longest and best of all oral narrative songs."[23]
These were the first texts, in the late eighth century. From then
on, they were recited on various occasions by rhapsodes in
competition, while simultaneously the aoedic (bardic) oral tradition continued, ignoring the text, and some of its purveyors
claimed descent from Homer, the Homeridae, and sang the
songs (like all oral bards) the same way—only better.[24]

If one asks how this tradition terminated, my guess is that
eventually it became unpopular because it was eclipsed by the
official performances of Homer given by the rhapsodes who
produced the real text (*not* interpolated) and that gradually it
died away in the provinces, where perhaps recorded versions,
also dictated, became the basis for the so-called City Texts,
which the Alexandrine scholars knew. But that is another whole
argument. The text we have is, I believe, really quite close to
what Homer sang, and the chief difficulties in it, if they are due
to any post-Homeric activities, are due to those of schoolmasters
and scholars, from the schoolmaster who told Alcibiades that he
had a copy of Homer corrected by himself, to the most recent of
the Neo-Analysts.

21. Whitman, *Homer*, pp. 73ff.; see H. T. Wade-Gery, *The Poet of the
Iliad* (Cambridge, 1952) ch. 1, esp. pp. 14–18.
22. Lord, pp. 156–57.
23. Ibid., p. 153.
24. Cf. the remark in the much-discussed scholium to Pindar, *Nemean* 2.
1e (A. B. Drachmann, ed., *Scholia vetera in Pindari carmina*, vol. 3 [Leip-
zig, 1927], p. 31), that Cinaethus and his followers, in contrast to the
Homeridae, "did much damage" to the poetry of Homer (ἐλυμήναντο
δὲ αὐτῇ πάνυ), a statement that suggests, at least, that there was a known
text in existence for them to damage.

5. Antigone and the
Nature of Nature

Ever since Hegel, every kind of antinomy has been invoked to define the forces that conflict in Sophocles' *Antigone*. [1] It has been called a conflict between divine law and state law, family right and *polis* right, individual and state, democracy and oligarchy, aristocracy and democracy *megalopsychia* and *sophrosyne*, and so on down a long colonnade of stiff abstractions, until we think we have before us no longer a drama, but a treatise by a German philosopher of the nineteenth century—logical, rigid, and monolithic, but murky withal and a source of permanent rancor. Yet, oddly enough, the most crucial intellectual antinomy of Sophocles' own day has seldom been applied—the *nomos-physis* debate, the controversy that arose in the fifth century from the realization that the customs and statutes of man's social structures were often at odds with the demands and needs of human nature. The *nomos-physis* antinomy applies to the *Antigone* in a most illuminating and provocative way, for it reveals the play not in the light of a one-to-

1. See G. W. F. Hegel, *Lectures on the Philosophy of Religion*, trans. Spiers and Sanderson (London, 1895), 2. 264; *Lectures on Aesthetics*, trans. Osmaston (London, 1920), 1. 293 and 2. 215. Hegel's discussion of the *Antigone* is available in A. and H. Paolucci, eds., *Hegel on Tragedy* (Garden City, N.Y., 1962), pp. 68, 73–74, 133, 147, 178, 186, 197, 279–81, 360. See also L. A. MacKay, "Antigone, Coriolanus and Hegel," *Transactions of the American Philological Association* 93 (1962):166–74.

one clash of irreconcilable opposites, but as involved in a subtler
exploration of the true meaning of these concepts, both of
which could imply many things.[2] This approach, through the
crux of fifth-century intellectual history, especially through the
physis side of it, brings a more rewarding critical focus to
Sophocles' great work and one more congenial to its poetry. For
the *Antigone* is a poem, not a treatise on law; it is a poem on
nature, dealing incidentally with the laws of a land, and ultimately with the nature of the only laws that can be called true.

Antigone's most famous speech is, of course, the one in de-
fense of the laws of Zeus (450–60). It is not always agreed what
she means by the laws of Zeus. All she says is that they are
unwritten, unfailing, eternal, of obscure origin, and of greater
authority than Creon's. Whatever other unwritten laws there
may have been, there can be little doubt that Antigone here
means some kind of natural law; in the phrase of Aristotle, who
quotes the passage, she means, "Law according to nature; for
there exists a universal right and wrong," τὸν κατὰ φύσιν
νόμον. ἔστι γὰρ . . . φύσει κοινὸν δίκαιον καὶ ἄδικον.[3]
Such law is necessarily unwritten; we meet a similar idea in
Pericles' remark about laws "which, though unwritten, involve
an acknowledged shame,"[4] though these may be not strictly
laws of "nature," but simply principles of conduct commonly
agreed on by civilized people. The real conflict between human
law and nature, however, is felt keenly in the Sophist Antiphon's
phrase: "Many things that are considered legally right are hostile
to [human] nature," πολλὰ τῶν κατὰ νόμον δικαίων
πολεμίως τῇ φύσει κεῖται.[5] This statement, roughly contemporary with the *Antigone*, or only a little later, summarizes,

2. See, for instance, Socrates' quizzical distortion of the terms in Plato,
Gorgias 488b2–489b6.

3. *Rhet.* 1. 13. 2; cf. R. C. Jebb, *Sophocles, The Plays and Fragments*, pt.
3, *Antigone*, 2d ed. (Cambridge, 1900) ad loc.

4. Thuc. 2. 37. 3.

5. Antiphon the Sophist, frag. B44, col. 2, 26–30 DK.

in its simplest form, the problem dramatized between Antigone
and Creon. Antiphon, moreover, strongly favored the claims of
physis, which he saw as constituting Truth; Antigone, as we
shall see, concurs, though in a way found only in the fiery ethos
of Sophoclean heroism, not in the philosophers. For her, there
is unassailable authority in natural bonds, and she asserts this
belief to Creon, though the word she uses is not *physis*, but
ἄγραπτα νόμιμα, "unwritten laws." The intensity of her personal feelings causes her to emerge as the defender of what she
deems nature's inherent, immutable, and, therefore, divine
order, to be maintained at cost of life in the face of conflicting
human (or, in this case, inhuman) decrees. Though she acts,
certainly, on a principle, the principle is felt not as a remote
moral imperative, but as the true and proper structure of her
own authentic self (*physis*), to be expressed and vindicated by
action. In a fine line she makes this clear: οὔτοι συνέχθειν,
ἀλλὰ ουμφιλεῖν ἔφυν, "My nature is to join in love, not hate"
(523). The love of which she speaks is the inborn bond between
relatives; she identifies herself with this love. She hopes, too,
for a similar response from Ismene (38), but it is not to come;
Ismene's view of her own "nature" is that it is "helpless": δρᾶν
ἔφυν ἀμήχανος, (79); cf. γυναῖχ᾽ ὅτι / ἔφυμεν ("because we
were born women," 61–62). In a later scene, Haemon, too,
seeks to elicit from his father some natural feeling, but it is clear
that the two have somewhat opposed notions of "natural" obligation. Haemon, for instance, regards intelligence as a natural
gift, engendered by the gods in men (683): the man who is full
of knowledge, he says, has the "natural" claim to "eldership"
(πρεσβεύειν, 720–21); actual age is of less moment. He emphasizes also the "naturalness" of his concern for his father
(688). But he is countered by a quite different outlook on the
meaning of family ties: in Creon's view, when a man has children, he finds fulfillment primarily in their obedience to pater-
nal orders (641ff.); if they are not obedient, they are "useless
growths," and he has bred himself trouble. Creon vows that he

will not nurture unruly kindred, but cut off what cannot be kept in its place; let Antigone, if she will, call on Zeus Synaimos, guardian of family ties! (cf. 485–86.) Nature, with all the ties of love and kinship (*philia*) that it implies, is to be subdued and subordinated to the civil hierarchy. Such varying attitudes toward nature were abroad in Sophocles' time; one thinks of Thucydides' account of the differing views of Spartans and Athenians toward human nature.[6] Antigone's difference with Creon, which she states as irreconcilable (501), is basically of the same kind, a difference about the nature of nature, so to speak; throughout, her use of such words as φύω, "be by nature", φιλέω, "love," and the strong αὐτάδελφος, "my very own sister," in line 1, declares her allegiance to nature and her belief in it as the basis of all law in the world.[7]

Yet Sophocles was not advancing "natural law" in any simplistic sense; least of all was he ignoring the contradictions and terrors of nature on the one hand or the claims of civilization on the other. The sophistic discovery that man was an animal, and a dangerous one, posed a new and serious threat to all the assumptions of civilization, and Sophocles knew this quite as well as did Antiphon or Euripides, whose dramas abound in chilling representations of "natural man." In placing Antigone on the side of nature, he had more in mind than a sophistic estimate of its human variety; he raised the question of the human potential at its fullest, as a phenomenon born of nature and nurtured on it and therefore committed to all that could be meant by man. He suggests that social institutions are at odds not only with the individual's needs, but even with the natural ground and essence of humanity itself, and he has much to say about that essence in the character of his most splendid heroine.

6. Cf. Thuc. 1. 84 and 2. 40.
7. Cf. Creon's ἀδελφὰ τῶνδε (192), "sisters of these decrees)."

After beginning his drama, as he usually does, with action, conflict, and complex involvement, Sophocles presently arrives at what seems to be a still point, an almost philosophical reflection on man, in the famous first stasimon (332–75). This ode, usually called the Ode on Man, though it could equally well be called the Ode on Nature, has been read as a hymn of tribute to human achievement, culminating in civilization, the *polis*. Certainly the Promethean spirit, *homo faber*, is paramount. But there are ambiguities throughout. The very word δεινόν sounds an ambiguous note at the opening:[8] δεινόν very seldom means "wondrous," or "wonderful," as it is always translated; its meaning is "dreadful," or "formidable." "Clever" or "compelling" marks a more neutral meaning in the idiom δεινὸς λέγειν, "fearfully clever at speaking," in which, however, the real force of δεινός as "fearful" has become weakened by context. Generally the word implies danger, not reassurance. When we look at man's actions in the poem, it is clear that they, too, are, at the very least, equivocal, if telling and frightening. We begin with seafaring, proverbial for folly and impiety; then comes the image of plowing, cast in terms of "wearing away the greatest of divinities, Earth," a phrase that connotes the creative struggle with nature, but also the end of the Golden Age, after the fall of man, when toil first became necessary. Then come the hunting images, hunting of birds and beasts: we are reminded of the violent beast imagery of the *parodos*, where the Argive eagle confronts the Theban dragon with deadly blood-lust (110–27). These are the sanguinary struggles man's conquest entails, the savagery of nature that can never be expunged. Then come "speech and thought, swift as wind"—man's best

8. Heidegger recognized this ambiguity in his overschematized but interesting essay, "The Ode on Man in Sophocles' *Antigone*," in *An Introduction to Metaphysics*, trans. R. Manheim (New Haven, 1959), reprinted in Thomas Woodward, ed., *Sophocles: A Collection of Critical Essays* (Englewood Cliffs, N.J., 1966) pp. 86–100. See also MacKay, p. 174n.13.

moment so far—and finally, civic institutions. Here one is
struck by the phrase ἀστυνόμους ὀργάς (355–56), which is
generally translated as the "temper for ruling cities"; yet ὀργή is
a word not inevitably bound to favorable connotations,[9] but
quite as susceptible to double interpretation as what has gone
before; it usually means "rage." Then come the most ambiguous
words of all: παντοπόρος·ἄπορος ἐπ᾽ οὐδὲν ἔρχεται τὸ
μέλλον; man is "all-inventive and approaches nothing that shall
come to him without resource" (360–61). Or does it mean,
"All-inventive man comes resourceless to the nothingness
that is his future"? The Greek works equally well either way,
and what follows in the last stanza does not clarify; it says only
that man suffers both good and ill by turns, and that he who
reveres justice stands high in his city, while he who does not is
ἄπολις—a man of no city. The vigorous and promising beginning of the poem has simmered down to a hesitant whisper.
Sophocles seems to have combined two traditions about early
man, both of which were current in his time: the tradition of
progress and achievement, perhaps immediately due to Protagoras, and the old Hesiodic tradition of decline and fall. The
result is an ode that presents the Promethean spirit, and its
conquest of nature, in a light of uncertainty, at least; perhaps
even of inadequacy.

The Promethean is one approach by which to assess man's
relation with nature. But there is another view, a far more subtle
one, which presents the human spirit as being not so much the
conqueror of nature as a uniter of its forces within itself, less the
creator of "city-ruling tempers" and all that is meant by law in
that sense and more the unifier of the natural world in a culminating consciousness of *its* laws. This is a process of

---

9. Cf. MacKay's suggestion (p. 174,n.13) that the phrase could mean
"police-department tempers." Ὀργή certainly more often implies bad temper
than good, as in *Antigone* 280. [See C. Segal, "Sophocles' Praise of Man and
the Conflicts of the *Antigone*" in Woodard, p. 71.]

moralization of what is "naturally" given, which is the real heroic achievement in Sophocles' tragic structure.

The scene in the *Antigone* which points most clearly to this heroic moral realtionship between man and nature is the scene in which Antigone is apprehended, after she has appeared in the midst of a great dust storm, standing and lamenting beside her brother's body. To understand this relationship, we must tackle an old problem, one long debated by critics of the play, the so-called "double burial." It has been called an uninteresting question, and even the meticulous Sir Richard Jebb gave little attention to it. But properly understood it leads us to the central issues of Sophoclean heroism.

Antigone seems to have buried her brother not once, but twice. Sometime between the end of the prologue and the first entrance of the guard, the body had been sprinkled with fine dust, which constituted a symbolic, but sacramentally adequate burial.[10] The guard, who reports this fact to Creon, is sent back with threats to find the culprit. He and his fellows sweep the dust from the body and mount watch over it from a nearby hill. A sudden dust storm arises, blinding them temporarily, and when it clears, they see Antigone in the act of bringing more dust, lamenting, and pouring the triple libations for the dead. They apprehend her, accuse her of both burials—which she apparently admits (434–35)—and bring her before Creon. Now, deeply devoted as Antigone was to her brother, and deeply as she was outraged by the edict that refused him burial, presum-

---

10. See I. Errandonea, "La dobla visita de Antigone al cadaver de su hermano Polinices," *Estudios Clásicos* 3 (1955):111–20, for the theory that Antigone had already sprinkled the dust before the play opens. There is no evidence for this theory in the play, and if it were the case, one might have expected Antigone to mention her act. As for what constitutes ritually adequate burial, Jebb, ad 429, is satisfied with the evidence of Horace, *Carm.* 1. 28. 35, that a sprinkling of dust is sufficient. One need not go so far afield: the answer is in the guard's words, 245–46, θάψας βέβηκε, "someone buried the body and went away," and Creon certainly considers it a burial.

ably one burial was enough. It was enough, at least, to enrage Creon, as a full breach of the decree. Why did it have to be done twice?

The answers scholars have offered have been many, all different, mostly suffering from the rigor mortis of literalism.[11] Jebb (*ad* 429) contents himself by suggesting that on her first visit Antigone had not brought the libations. But how odd of Sophocles to give his heroine such a pointless strain of forgetfulness! If the libations were crucial, by what inexplicable absentmindedness could the intense Antigone neglect them? And if they were not crucial, why did she bother with them at all? Jebb's solution is out of character for Antigone. But it is better than the wild-eyed suggestion that Antigone was just naturally a martyr and wanted to get caught; having failed to find herself apprehended the first time, she tried again.[12] Such an interpretation transforms the heroic defiance into a neurosis. Nor does it make sense to say that Ismene performed the first burial, as has been argued by W. H. D. Rouse.[13] It is true, she says that she did (536) in a moment of what is clearly hysteria (cf. λυσσῶσαν, "raging mad," 492); but she is soon persuaded that she did not. And if Creon, who says twice that he would like to kill both sisters (488, 769), becomes convinced of Ismene's inno-

11. For surveys see Holger Friis Johansen, "Sophocles 1939–1959," *Lustrum* 7 (1963):186; more recently, Marsh McCall, "Divine and Human Action in Sophocles: The Two Burials of the *Antigone*," *Yale Classical Studies* 22 (1972):103–117. [D. A. Hester, "Sophocles the Unphilosophical," *Mnemosyne* 24 (1971):25ff. (bibliography, 48–54); Charles Segal, *Tragedy and Civilization: An Interpretation of Sophocles*, Martin Classical Lectures 26 (Cambridge, Mass., 1981), pp. 159–60n.25 with 442–43.]

12. See McCall, p. 105n.17; Gilbert Norwood, *Greek Tragedy* (Boston, 1920), p. 140, describes Antigone as "splendid through perverse valor. . . . She throws away her life, *and with no possible confidence that her brother will in the end be buried*" (Norwood's italics). Norwood's remarks seem to me unclear, but perhaps he was suggesting something in the nature of a martyr complex.

13. W. H. D. Rouse, "The Two Burials in *Antigone*," *Classical Review* 25 (1911):40–42.

cence, we can spare ourselves the unedifying picture of timid Ismene, after refusing to help her sister, sneaking out, burying the body, and then letting Antigone, a poor second, take all the punishment.

Many other recourses have been tried: to bury Polyneices once was not enough of a *hamartia* for a Sophoclean protagonist; two burials, however, constitute real defiance of law, and therefore due and sufficient cause for destruction.[14] One may ignore that theory, along with what is the easiest answer of all, that Sophocles was simply guilty of a dramatic error.[15] G. M. Kirkwood comes closer to the point by arguing that Sophocles has here used a "dramatic device" with quite specific intentions.[16] Indeed he did, but Kirkwood's explanation, that Sophocles irrationally put in two separate burials because he wanted two separate results from it, Antigone's defiance of Creon *and* Antigone's capture, seems hardly consistent with the poet's celebrated dramaturgical skill and elegance. In Kirkwood's scheme, there is too much "dramatic device" and not enough meaning.

Finally, we must mention S. M. Adams's theory that the first burial was not performed by Antigone at all, but by the gods.[17] The suggestion has been called preposterous,[18] but it actually finds much support right at the outset, in the impressive words of the guard, as he begins his tremulous report to the king. Creon asks, "Who has dared this deed?" The guard answers:

14. Minnie Keyes Flickinger, The Ἁμαρτία of Sophocles' Antigone, Iowa Studies in Classical Philology 2 (Iowa City, 1935).

15. J. E. Harry, *Studies in Sophocles*, University of Cincinnati Studies, 2d ser. 7 (Cincinnati, 1911).

16. G. M. Kirkwood, A *Study of Sophoclean Drama*, Cornell Studies in Classical Philology 31 (Ithaca, N.Y., 1958), p. 70.

17. First in *Classical Review* 45 (1931):110–11; then in *Phoenix* 9 (1955):47–62; finally in *Sophocles the Playwright* (Toronto, 1957), ch. 3.

18. By Johansen, p. 186, and by many others. There is nothing inherently "preposterous" about the gods performing funeral rites for those left unburied; cf. *Iliad* 24. 610–12. Again, for a full account of scholarly reactions to Adams's theory, see McCall, pp. 103–4, who argues cogently in its support.

> I know nothing; there was neither stroke of spade
> Nor mattock; no earth turned, but dry and hard,
> Unbroken even by the print of wheels
> Or wagon; whoever did it left no trace.
> But when the first watch of the day pointed
> And showed us, baffled wonder gripped us all.
> The corpse had disappeared, not buried, no,
> But skimmed with dust, as if someone shunned his curse.
>
> [249–56]

The total absence of wheel-prints, or any other evidence of human presence, certainly points to some obscure agency, for we know that Antigone was not concerned with hiding her traces. The poet must mean something by inserting and elaborating this mystifying feature. Adams therefore concluded that the perpetrators of the first funeral were the gods.

The chorus's first thought is a similar one, that the deed was θεήλατον (278), "impelled by the gods" or "wrought by the gods," as Jebb interprets. The chorus says:

> My lord, my thoughts are prompting me long since
> To wonder if this deed were wrought by gods.
>
> [278–79]

Given the guard's description of the circumstances, the conclusion is almost inevitable; but Creon (like Adams's critics) finds it preposterous:

> Silence, before you choke me full with rage
> Uttering such things! You've turned a doddering fool.
> It is intolerable to hear you speak
> Of any gods' compassion for this corpse.
> What? Bury him like an honored benefactor
> Who came with fire against their pillared shrines
> To burn them and their sacred offerings,
> Their very land, and scatter their observance?
> Do the gods, in your view, so honor crime?
>
> [280–88]

It is a well-known dramatic technique to build tension and
heighten the importance of an element in a play by introducing
conflict over it. In the first scene of *Hamlet*, Horatio's brief
"Tush, 'twill not appear" builds and enlarges the entrance of the
ghost. What people argue over in a play lingers in the mind,
and here we are meant, obviously, not to dismiss (with Creon)
the possibility of some kind of divine agency in the first burial,
but to think about it. Later on in the play, Teiresias's report of
the shrieking birds and sputtering flames of the rejected sacrifice
leaves us in no doubt whatever that the gods have taken an
interest, and an angry one, in the unburied corpse of
Polyneices.

So far, Adams's observations appear to be well founded in the
text, and in accord with the play's general tenor. The rest of his
argument—that the gods, though feeling protective about the
corpse, want Antigone to get caught—finds no support in the
play and needs no reply. But we must ask whether the gods
themselves actually performed the funeral or if Adams's interpretation is too simple. The *locus classicus* for gods burying
mortals is Book 24 of the *Iliad*, in which they bury the children
of Niobe. On that occasion, no human takes part, least of all
repeats the gods' work. If Sophocles had wanted us to understand that the gods themselves had buried Polyneices, he could
have made that clear; then there would have been no need for
Antigone, and we would have had a different play. Instead, he
only made mysterious suggestions. Besides, the gods themselves
are scarce in Sophocles and are felt rather as symbols moving
behind the immediate panorama of character, deed, and suffering than as simple agents of justice of vengeance. We would do
better, therefore, not to look to the gods, but to Nature herself as
having joined in the burial of Polyneices.

It has seldom been said, but it could scarcely be denied, that
the most central dramatic image of the *Antigone* is the image of
inverted nature.[19] Teiresias is quite explicit when, in the mo-

19. [See T. F. Hoey, "Inversion in the *Antigone*: A Note," *Arion* 9
(1970):337–45.]

ment of revealing to Creon the true nature of his actions, he
states:

> You have turned all things on their heads, scornfully
> Lodging a living soul within a tomb
> And keeping here, stripped of rites and gods
> Below, a graveless and unhallowed corpse!
>   [1068–71]

The first half of the play is overshadowed by recurrent pictures
of the unburied dead, the second half by the image of Antigone
immured alive. Toward the end, the entire horror is sharply
focused upon Creon himself, to whom the messenger refers
pointedly as an ἔμψυχον νεκρόν, "living corpse" (1167). To
those who believe that there was justice in the original edict of
Creon against the interment of Polyneices, or his punishment of
Antigone, be it said only that by the end of the play there is no
one left alive, least of all Creon himself, who can be found to
praise the violation of nature. Teiresias's words are final on the
subject, and Nature herself, though voiceless, reponds in action.

She responds with a dust storm of terrifying violence, which
the guard describes in words that suggest the supernatural
(415–21). It belongs, in fact, to the same literary species as the
eerie vortex of mist and dust that covers the corpse of Patroclus
in the seventeenth book of the *Iliad*. Yet it is still a natural
phenomenon; it is not a direct intervention by the gods, but a
symbolic extension into nature of Antigone's handful of dust, a
manifestation of Antigone's relation to natural laws. As defender
of these, she is supported by Nature herself, and this inner
sustenance finds an outer symbol in the natural dust storm, after
which Antigone covers the body (417–31). In the same way,
Creon's violation of nature finds an outer symbol in the shrieking birds and rejected sacrifice. The dust storm falls into the
category of an omen, a token of the true state of things as they
are about to be revealed in the play's action; it is the walking

ghost, the symbol of the "hid impostume." But nature, for the Greeks, and particularly for Antigone, is divine, and the chorus, in tentatively calling the deed θεήλατον, "impelled by God," has told something: that Nature and Antigone are one in the act of burial. The first dust is a symbolic predicate of Antigone's deed.

We need not ask how many dust storms there were, or how many trips Antigone made to the corpse. The action must be looked upon as a single whole, described in two phases, so that the storm in which Antigone actually appears may not be taken as simply casual weather. There were two agencies, human and divine, but the two were one in Antigone's act, without which the gods could not have acted. They act through nature, nature in general and Antigone's nature. There was only one burial, told twice.

Sophocles' rhetoric in describing the storm reiterates, in such phrases as οὐράνιον ἄχος (417) and θεία νόσος (421), the feeling of uncanniness created by the earlier scene with the unexplained dust that covered the body (256). These phrases should not be rendered, as Jebb translates them, simply as "trouble in the sky" and "heaven-sent plague," respectively. They connote the "disease" of violated nature and divine abhorrence. This is no ordinary storm:

> καὶ τότ᾽ ἐξαίφνης χθονὸς
> τυφὼς ἀείρας σκηπτόν, οὐράνιον ἄχος,
> πίμπλησι πεδίον, πᾶσαν αἰκίζων φόβην
> ὕλης πεδιάδος, ἐν δ᾽ ἐμεστώθη μέγας
> αἰθήρ· μύσαντες δ᾽ εἴχομεν θείαν νόσον.

> Then suddenly from the earth
> A whirlwind lifted dust to anguished heaven;
> It filled the plain, torturing every lock
> Of the forest where it stretched away, the great upper
> Air was stuffed; we muffled up, bearing divine affliction.
> [417–21]

Merely in point of metrics, lines 418–20 are startling, with their bold resolutions. Sophoclean metrics tend to support meaning, and here surely the rare succession of tribrachs reflects and emphasizes an unparalleled irregularity in nature.[20] The imagery of the passage, too, is remarkable. The phrase πᾶσαν αἰκίζων φόβην/ὕλης πεδιάδος, "torturing every lock of the forest where it stretched away" (419–20), conjures the picture of nature as a woman lamenting and tearing her hair, while a few lines later Antigone's cries of lament are compared to those of bereft bird. The two images complement each other, underlining the identity of Antigone and nature.[21]

There is one passage, however, which may seem to deny the whole theory that the gods were responsible for the first burial. The guard reports that Antigone, when arrested and accused of committing both burials, pleaded guilty:

> And we accused her of the former deed
> And this; and she just stood, denying nothing.
>
> [434–35]

At first glance, this certainly looks as if Antigone acknowledges two trips and two burials. Yet that is not what is actually said, and the fact that it is implied only serves to remind us of the mysterious first dust. One simple answer to this objection has been made:[22] the guard and his fellows thought some *person* had committed the former burial, and it was reasonable for them to infer, after catching her in the "second" act, that it was Antigone. They were anxious to account for all infractions, and Antigone would not, perhaps, bother to deny a charge that was incomprehensible to her when she was caught red-handed in an identical one. Small puzzlements matter little in great

---

20. But cf. *Ajax* 459–61.
21. Cf. Aesch. *Prom.* 406–7 for comparable imagery of Nature lamenting in sympathy for Prometheus.
22. McCall, p. 109.

moments, and Antigone had no desire to hide her deed. But the best answer is that in the symbolic scheme Antigone and the dust storm of nature are indistinguishable. What matters is that dust fell both from the divine and troubled sky and from the human hand of Antigone. The concurrence of her moral nature and of nature at large in the same deed is what matters for a drama whose controlling action is the sacramental sprinkling of funeral dust.

But the natural, or supernatural, dust storm, the οὐράνιον ἄχος, is not all. In the great *kommos*, in which she is led away to death, predicates of nature and divinity continue to surround Antigone. Lamenting the loss of her marriage and her shattered youth, she sings that she will "marry Acheron" (816). This image of the "bride of death"—so archetypal that it seems the universal possession of all poets—leads on to her vision of herself as Niobe (823–33), another archetype used long ago by Homer in the closing of the *Iliad* to encompass that ultimate pitch of grief which, though frozen and immobilized, still pours out tears—a weeping stone: ἔνθα λίθος περ ἐοῦσα θεῶν ἐκ κήδεα πέσσει, "There stone though she is she broods on her griefs from the gods" (*Il.* 24. 617). The famous "Niobe" of Mt. Sipylus was a natural rock formation, according to Pausanias, which from a distance looked like a seated woman, bent over weeping; Antigone's words seem to describe Niobe's fate as something like that of a lean-to built in the woods and left, until it becomes overgrown and all but undiscoverable:

I have heard of the Phrygian sojourner, daughter of Tantalus,
Who perished in grief by the peak of Mount Sipylus,
Overwhelmed by a tight growth of rock like ivy.
Rains and snows never leave her, men say, and under her weeping brows
Her bosom is wet with tears. Most like to her
The *daimon* now lays me to sleep.

[823–33]

Niobe's petrifaction is seen not as an instantaneous metamor-
phosis, but as a gradual absorption into the processes of nature,
as of something growing into the true shape of its identity.
Antigone too, groping to understand her fate under some
paradigm, some mythic pattern, feels herself being absorbed by
the stone of her tomb, as she too moves into the fixity of myth.
To see it as process, or growth "like ivy," is to see it as "natural,"
even though elsewhere in the play the manner of her death,
burial alive, figures as a violation of nature commensurate with
leaving a corpse unburied. But through the symbolic scheme
Antigone transforms her grotesque punishment into a further
extension of her identity with natural order, as well as with
Niobe, the paradigm of incorrigible natural love. In reply, the
chorus, hesitant and half-comprehending as all Sophoclean
choruses, yet sympathetic, concedes that her life and death do
align with the ἰσόθεοι, the "demigods," of old. Antigone rejects their words as a mockery, an overplaying of her comparison with Niobe; they are, nonetheless, true, even though she,
like every true hero, is too human and alone to be consoled by
the thought of her own greatness.

Antigone's final lines before she is led away are given over to a
restatement of the justice of her cause [937–43], broken by one
brief outcry at the horror of death (933).[23] But now the realm of
nature, which had attained subtly symbolic force in the dust
storm and mythic permanence in the rocky figure of Niobe,
becomes the burden of an ode by the chorus, the fourth stasimon. This poem has been expounded by scholars with such
exuberant diversity that it is manifest that none of them knows
why it is there.

Most interpretations recognize that the chorus draws some
vague analogies between Antigone and three other persons who
were imprisoned, but beyond that the similarities fade. Danae

23. [Whitman followed the manuscripts and the scholia in attributing
933–34 to Antigone; Lehrs (followed by Pearson in the Oxford Classical Text)
assigned 933–34 to the chorus.]

was shut in a brazen tower, where she became the mother of
Perseus by Zeus in the form of a golden shower; Lycurgus, the
fierce king who attacked Dionysus and his Maenads, was imprisoned in a cave and later came to worse grief; finally,
Cleopatra, the rejected wife of King Phineus of Salmydessus,
was locked up and her children blinded by Phineus's new
spouse. These characters, one a famous heroine, one an impious criminal, and one an innocent sufferer, bear little resemblance to each other and none to Antigone, save for noble birth
and a term in jail. If Sophocles was looking only for pedantic
parallels, he perhaps succeeded; Jebb explains that all three were
caught by the power of fate, and Kirkwood talks about the
poem's "lyrical relevance," without saying what it is; *alii alia.* [24]

The varying interpretations have come from looking at *why*
Danae, Lycurgus, and Cleopatra were imprisoned, instead of
looking at *where*; and since the ode is somewhat neglected, it
may be worthwhile to review it:

Beautiful Danae endured,
Lost to the light of the sky, locked in brass-bound halls;
Hid in a tomb vaulted chamber, caught fast;
Yet she was born to honor, Daughter,
And fostered the seed of Zeus poured down in a stream of gold.
But fatal power is great and dread;
Nor wealth nor war, nor tower eludes it,
Nor black ships, buffeted hard at sea.

King of Edonia,
The son of Dryas, sharp-tempered Lycurgus was walled
By Bacchus in rocky bondage, with all his taunting rage;
There did his fearful, luxuriant fierceness
Slowly distill away: he learned to know
The god he had touched with his mocking tongue.
For he tried to quell the god-filled women, the Bacchic fire,
And stirred the hate of the Muses who love the flute.

24. Kirkwood, p. 211n.38.

By the Dark Rocks where the two seas meet,
Are the Cliffs of the Bosporus, and Salmydessus;
Where once Ares who guards his city
Witnessed the cursed thrust, struck by a savage stepmother,
The sons of Phineus, blinded,
And the sightless eyeballs crying for vengeance!
Children torn by a bloody hand,
And the points of a shuttle.

Wasting in sorrow and pain, they wailed,
Born of a mother cast out from wedlock;
Yet she, who could trace her seed
To the ancient-born house of Erechtheus,
Grew as a girl in far-distant caves,
In the whirl of her father's storms,
Daughter of Boreas, swift as a colt on the dizzy slopes,
Child of gods; yet even on her,
The long-lived fates bore hard.
Daughter.

[944–87]

We may be permitted to see more than fate in all this. Three
of the four elements take part in it (sea, sky, rocks), together with
a number of gods (Zeus, Dionysus, Ares twice, the Muses,
Boreas), as well as the three great phases of organic nature—
birth, marriage, wasting away. As in the Niobe passage, natural
processes and divinity meet in a kind of implied large scheme of
things whose exact workings, however, are left undefined.
Sophocles calls it by the word μοῖρα, "fate," which means
only that these things happened. But the center of this
panoramic context is the *place* where the prisoners were confined, the cave. Danae's prison is not actually called a cave, but
it is called a τυμβήρης θάλαμος, a "tomblike chamber"
(947), even more specifically a tomblike marriage-chamber,
which closely resembles Antigone's invocation of the cave in
which she is to be immured:

ὦ τύμβος, ὦ νυμφεῖον, ὦ κατασκαφῆς
οἴκησις αἰείφρουρος ...

my tomb, my bridal chamber, my underground habitation,
always under guard ...

[891–92]

The chorus has picked up Antigone's words, along with her
statement that she will marry Acheron, and transferred them to
the confinement of Danae, whose prison turned out to be, in
fact, a marriage-chamber. Despite the tradition about the brazen tower, which the ode actually mentions, one imagines
Danae in a rocky, tomblike cave similar to Antigone's. Lycurgus
too, was shut in a πετρώδης δεσμός, "rocky dungeon" (957).
The prison of Cleopatra and her children is not described,
though again one tends to picture a cavern of some kind. Suddenly, however, at the end of the ode, we are transported back-
ward in time to the girlhood of Cleopatra, when she was growing
up among the whirling storms of her father Boreas "in distant
caves."

    Caves in Greece, though sometimes used as places of con-
finement, were actually shrines, normally sacred to the
Nymphs, or Pan, the spirits of nature. It is animism in its
simplest form for natural phenomena to breed gods of nature.
Caves are nature's secret spots where a mortal may meet with
divinities. Homer tells us of a cave of the Nymphs in Ithaca,
which had two entrances:

> There are tall looms of stone, whereon the Nymphs
> Weave sea-purple garments, a wonder to see;
> There is water ever flowing, there are two portals also,
> One that faces the north, where mortal men may enter,
> And one for gods, opening southward; no man
> Enters there; it is the way of immortals.
>
> [Od. 13. 107ff.]

Not all caves, of course, have two entrances, though the oracular cavern on Mount Cynthos in Delos does, and so does the cave of Philoctetes in Sophocles' play of that name. The two gates, discriminately marked, simply emphasize the meaning of a cave as the point of contact between gods and men. So it is in this ode; the three characters in the caves find themselves in the presence of divinity, after one fashion or another: Danae with Zeus, Lycurgus with Dionysus—and Cleopatra? Her case is more complex, for she had grown up in caves, the daughter of the North Wind, a divine child of nature, while her confinement and suffering came only afterward. But the motif of the cave is there, and reference to Cleopatra's happy early life cannot be taken as an irrelevancy, as it would be if the point of this ode were simply imprisonment.

Actually, this choral song is a poetic exploration of a cave, *the* archetypal cave, which is both womb and tomb, a place of darkness and of enlightenment, both prison and the natural dwelling place of the free life of gods and winds. It is the place of the immemorial, mysterious oppositions of glory, as for Danae, and abasement, as for Lycurgus. In the poem's structure, these two receive but one stanza each; Cleopatra, however, has two, in which the oppositions of the cave symbolism are polarized, in a single lifetime, into two separate caves, one of imprisonment and unjust suffering, the other of the freedom of the gods.

After what the choristers suggested in the *kommos* about Antigone's sharing in the dignity of the demigods, it is a simple step for them to see her entombment now in the light of mythic paradigms of heroic glory and heroic agony, which are the dialectic of tragedy. They are the terms in which a tragic hero meets the gods, and that meeting, in a play having so much to do with nature, is decorously located in a cave, which is the place of isolation, suffering, and union with divinity. It is hard to see how this chorus, which has often been held to be irrelevant, could have been written differently, or made more pointed.

The impious Lycurgus may seem to resist this interpretation, but for him, too, the cave was more than a prison; it was a cave of enlightenment, for he "learned to recognize" the god, ἐπέγνω... τὸν θεόν (961–62). His experience looks to that of the equally impious Creon, who recognized what he had done only when he went to the cave and saw. In the final analysis, the cave is the place of truth. It is here that Creon, who had divorced himself from all natural bonds, in rejecting his son's appeals and swearing that he would kill his niece even if she were the very closest of his kin, staggers under the full impact of violated nature's recoil, as Lycurgus felt the impact of Dionysus, the god of natural forces whom he reviled.

In the cave, too, Haemon and Antigone are united in a tragic, but true, marriage. Antigone repeatedly refers to her unmarried state, but calls her tomb a marriage-chamber; Cleopatra conversely, though married and a mother, is called ἀνύμφευτος (980), "cast out from wedlock," "unhappily married" (Jebb), literally "unwedded," a word selected more for Antigone's sake than for her own. When the messenger reports finally that Haemon has consummated τὰ νυμφικὰ τέλη... ἐν Ἅιδου δόμοις, "the marriage rites... in Hades' halls" (1240f.), Nature, however blunted, maimed, and deflected, has asserted herself with a kind of grim, ineluctable majesty that forces upon Creon, at last, his first natural feeling in the whole play—grief for his own family, destroyed by himself.

Despite this vindication of the power of natural bonds it would be an error to affect an exaggerated historical view, to see the tragedy as having to do with the ancient Greeks' special horror at the shedding of kindred blood or with the sanctified claims of the members of one's immediate family. Antigone's brother's corpse, though the direct cause of the action, is not the only central concern, nor is the term "natural bonds" so confined in its meaning. It seems to include all bonds that can be felt as human—in fact, all bonds of love. We have grown so used to thinking of the *Antigone* as a play in which a young

woman defies a king in a fight about law and have heard so
many time-honored red herrings about her "harshness," that
most scholars treat her as a person they would not like to know,
even if she was right. (It is an alarming commentary on classics
professors that many of them seem to be glad when she finally
gets walled up and close the book with evident relief at that
point.)

Fortunately, not all the characters in the play see Antigone in
this way, and its total structure contradicts such an all too
Creon-like view. We must also reckon with Haemon. Once
more, we have been told by generations of philologists that we
must not look on Haemon as anything like the young lover of
modern dramas—as if an ancient Greek would stoop to such a
thing! Sophocles, of course, has made his young man quite
above the passions and sentimentalities of youthful love; he is
the voice of reason, of a careful *sophrosyne* (moderation or
good sense), remarkable for his controlled and guarded approach to his father.[25] With such a father, he may well be
guarded, or try to be. When the scene between father and son is
over, however, Haemon, his cause lost and his bride con-
demned, leaves in a suicidal passion not generally associated
with reason, *sophrosyne*, or guarded control. He proceeds to
commit suicide, having first contemplated committing parricide. Romeo himself, though given to a more tender eloqu-
ence, did no more. The rhetorical convention is, of course,
different, but the action and suffering are timeless. Haemon is a
young man in love with the princess, his betrothed, and just
because he happens to be the first such character ever to be
staged in the history of Western drama is no excuse to try to read
out of him all the passion that Sophocles has put in.

As if to make sure that we do not, he concludes his scene with
an ode in celebration of erotic love. Again, interpreters have
been a little dismayed. Jebb implies that the chorus is apologiz-

25. [See Jebb, Introduction, xii–xiii, xxx; see also Kurt von Fritz,
"Haimons Liebe zu Antigone," *Philologus* 89 (1934):18–33, reprinted in
Antike und moderne Tragödie (Berlin, 1962), pp. 227–40.]

ing for Haemon's hot behavior on grounds that he is young. But neither the tone of the ode nor the chorus leader's earlier remark, that a young man takes grief hard (767), is apologetic. They sing only of the universal power of love, a conventional theme ever since the Homeric *Hymn to Aphrodite* and doubtless for a long time before that. What Sophocles says about it is also mostly conventional:

> Eros, unconquered in war, Eros you who fall in havoc
> On men's possessions, who sleep nightlong in a girl's soft cheeks,
> And roam over seas and pastoral steadings;
> None of immortals or men of a day
> Elude you, but run mad and possessed.
>
> [780–81]

So far, Sophocles seems to have said nothing extraordinary, perhaps, except for the romantic touch about love sleeping in a girl's cheek, which seems to be Sophocles' addition to an otherwise familiar text—love as invincible warrior, with power over men and gods, over land and sea, wreaker of havoc to men's material comforts, a source of madness. The poem continues (791ff.):

> Even the minds of the just you pervert to harm and wickedness

—still quite conventional—

> And even now you have stirred this strife in men who are kin

—referring specifically to the battle of words between Creon and his son, of course, but without any clearly committed judgment on the matter; it is only that love is the cause. Then comes the surprise:

> Bright desire in the eyes of a new young bride
> Sits victorious in empire at the side of the Great Laws.
>
> [795–800]

Is Sophocles really saying that? Jebb couldn't believe it; he would have liked to emend, but failed to find anything satisfactory. These lines, he says, "if sound . . . mean that the love inspired by the maiden's eyes is a power 'enthroned in sway by the side of the great laws.'"[26] That is, exactly, what is said, and what is meant. Jebb struggles on: "The great laws are those 'unwritten' *moral* laws [my italics] which most men feel and acknowledge [and he refers to Antigone's words at 454ff.]; here, esp., the law of loyalty to country, the law of obedience to parents." Yet the ode says nothing about country or parents; Creon talks about country and parents, by which he means mostly himself. The words μεγάλων θεσμῶν ("great laws") can refer only to the great unwritten laws of Antigone. Beside these solemnities, love (like it or not) is boldly enthroned in a winning image, the light in a young girl's eyes. Beauty and love, too, are laws of the world.

The juxtaposition looked frivolous to Jebb; he could not join Sophocles in placing love on an equal basis with what he calls the great "moral laws." Yet Antigone never exactly called her laws moral. They are moral to her, since morality is a human business, a human creation, and she herself had the power to see them as a moral obligation. Antigone does not *obey* a great moral law; she enacts one when she buries her brother out of love. It is too simple to say that her love for her brother is of a different kind from the bright, erotic desire in the eyes. It is different in mode, in import, and in what it leads to. But both kinds are equally built into the structure of the universe, both are πάρεδροι, "enthroned in sway" (Jebb), beside the Great Laws. Brotherly love has power to defy kingly edicts; erotic love has power, when balked, to disrupt all that seems settled and to set father and son at odds. That is a law of the universe, one of the great laws of nature.

Is this law moral? That would depend on how one acts upon

26. Jebb ad 797–98.

it. Haemon stops short of crime, though sorely tempted to kill his father; he slays himself in honor of his love for Antigone, and there is a kind of negative morality in his deed. The play is not Haemon's play, and we must not make more of his role than the poet does. But there is nothing in the ode, or elsewhere in the text, to indicate that Haemon is to be seen as an unregenerate son who should have bowed sweetly to his father's outrages against nature. Nor is it likely that, in an otherwise conventional poem on the power of Eros, Sophocles would have added the images of soft cheeks and shining eyes if he had wanted us to turn a disparaging gaze on the compelling beauty of young love.

If one were to say that the *Antigone* is all about love, one would not be far wrong; but it is a large love, many-faceted and immanent in the workings of the world. Though it is not quite the cosmogonic Eros of Hesiod or Empedocles—such a function would hardly fit the drama—it figures in the action as an ordering principle; more specifically as a principle, or force, that strews certain seeming-orders, such as the laws of Creon, in ruins. It enacts a moral order based upon itself as a law of the world.

The last line of the ode returns to a traditional expression:

> Resistless in play is divine Aphrodite.
> [799]

But by now, in the context established, one sees more than the smiling Homeric goddess with her wiles and witchcraft. Sophoclean choruses are hopelessly inept when they try to cast up in reasoned words the meaning of the tragic experience; but occasionally the poet gives them quick and partial insights that crystallize into images of underlying truths, as here into the scope and wonder of love.

And now, in the light of these lyrical portions of the play, its main action, the conflict between Antigone and Creon, may be seen within its surrounding framework of thought. Sophocles

was a man of his age, certainly; one might almost say, he was
the man of his age; for his response to the debate over *nomos*
and *physis*, if we may judge by the *Antigone*, was less partial
and more comprehensive than the views of others, whether
thinkers like Antiphon or fellow dramatists like Euripides. For
Sophocles' world view is a strongly metaphysical one, in that he
alone, of all those who followed Protagoras in believing that
man was the measure of all things, burningly felt man to be the
ontological center of the universe. When he saw the individual,
he saw the *hero*, not a helpless waif. He saw the hero not simply
as an individual of boundless energy and will, who sweeps all
before him, but as a moral center who creates law and builds
order around his own being, phoenix-like, out of his own ruins.

The Ode on Man, as we have seen, ends darkly. It is a vision
of Promethean man, man as conqueror of intransigent nature,
man as reasoner and builder of civilization, but somehow
trapped in the very need for conquest of the limitless, as empire
always demands greater empire. At the end of the poem, the
limits loom in view; there is also death, even for the Titan,
man; and nature wins at last. But Sophocles saw the further
range, beyond nature's ultimate victory, the range of the self. If
nature is to be conquered, it must be conquered in the self
ultimately, in order for the deathless forces of true being to
avail. It is in this inward struggle that heroism consists, and in it
alone is the source of moral power and valid law. Its motive is
love, and its mode is sacrifice. Its form is a journey into death,
guided by the law of the self's will to be. Antigone goes on such
a journey, and the chorus recognizes it:

> Not stricken by wasting ills, nor given
> To death paid home by the sword,
> You only of mortals, you go alone
> Yourself your law, alive into death.
> [819–22]

The chorus's word, αὐτόνομος, which Jebb translates as "mistress of your own fate," means, even more strongly, a law unto yourself, "yourself your own law."

By contrast, Creon has been the man of law, law seen superficially as mere established authority, a mindless, fundamentalist scheme of upper and lower, of command and obedience, Spartan in its rigidity, and tyrannical in its repressiveness; a travesty of civilization's presumption to have subdued all *physis* to *nomos*. Nature is not subdued; she responds with howling dust storms and screaming birds to the abominations of such an establishment, driving it to its own nemesis of self-destruction.

But Sophocles has done far more than show that Creon was wrong; the *Antigone* offers a more positive vision than the *Bacchae*. It shows a miraculous merging of nature and law in the figure of the heroine. The laws of nature are not moral, but Antigone's nature, consisting, as she says, of love, is a moralizing power that brings the natural world into unity with herself in a way so absolute that the gods themselves take notice. Being attracts being. The image of Antigone in the storm of dust, lamenting while the forest around her tears its hair, frames a powerful ontological symbol of man, not the Promethean conqueror of nature, but the heroic self in nature, at one with it, yet greater in its act of love and self-sacrifice.

This moment of vision, seen only by the guards, never by Creon, is both the moment of true identity for Antigone and the moment of true law. In it, the problem of *nomos* versus *physis*, law versus nature, has ceased to be an antinomy; it has found resolution and unison in the heroic moment, where the intellectual and the instinctual are made one by the release of a transcending love, wherein there can be no conflict between self and law, since both are born in the same instant of tragic time.

6. Aristophanes and the City:

$\overline{1}$

or Everybody

Aristophanes often praised the country, but his place was the city; he was immersed in it, exasperated by it, and unable to live or write without it. Scholars who have pinpointed the references behind his jibes and explained the facts behind his fantasies have dogmatized, firmly but divergently, about his real beliefs concerning what was good for Athens. But he has given them a hard time, for Aristophanes was not so ingenuous about his beliefs as his bland prescriptions might lead one to believe. Those who claim to discover his *parti pris* often seem to have labored in forgetfulness of Shelley's observation that it is only the lesser poets that have aimed directly at doing moral good and that "the effect of their poetry is diminished in exact proportion to the degree in which they compel us to advert to this purpose." Aristophanes was not a lesser poet, nor has the effect of his poetry been diminished by anything. One reason is that, at base, it is not the Athens of the historians that he was immersed in; not so much the Athens of Cleon, Hyperbolus, and other nightmares, as an Athens that had become the timeless, engulfing metropolis, itself the nightmare, felt in full impact perhaps for the first time in the war years of the late fifth century B.C. This was an Athens larger and more threatening than the sum of its formidable parts, the city as monster, not ultimately distinguishable, in its effect on the soul, from Horace's *fumum et opes strepitumque Romae*, "the smoke, wealth, and noise of Rome" (*Odes* 3. 29. 12) or T. S. Eliot's "Unreal" London (*The Wasteland*, III and IV). For a poet to be immersed in such a city calls for a special language, a poetry sensitive to the immediate, yet concerned for something more lasting and basic; and Aristophanes was not found wanting.

The city was a Greek invention. Before it, there were cities, of course, in Egypt, Mesopotamia, and Asia Minor, as well as in prehistoric Greece itself, but they were something else—great spectacular centers, some of them wonders of the world, no doubt, but architectural wonders, monuments to the towering self-admiration of kings. The classical Greek city-state was something more like a state of mind. It was the idea of a community, at once natural and artificial, in which people bound together by ethnic and family ties might live under a commonly recognized, though infinitely alterable, principle of law—custom law, statute law, tradition—the whole representing some kind of social contract aimed at "liberty." So much was true of any Greek city, however differently Athens, Sparta, Corinth, or Thebes might define liberty or construct a constitution to gain it. The main thing was the state of mind and that everybody was in it. The early theorists of the city conceived it as a trust, a communal possession of inestimable price, the matrix of identity and excellence for all its citizens. For Protagoras, justice and self-respect were its foundation stones. "The City educates the man," sang Simonides (frag. 53 Diehl), in the full swing of the state of mind. But by the late fifth century, among those who lived in Athens experiencing her daily advantages, challenges, and frustrations, the state of mind that professed law and aimed at liberty was heavily cross-hatched with the dark truth, that there is nothing like civilization to bring out the beast in man.

Pericles said that a city consists not of walls and ships, but of men (Thucydides 1. 143. 5), and Athens produced all kinds, including the various cheats, quacks, shysters, and entrepreneurs we have come to expect of a great urban center. In the cities of the Pharaohs, corruption must certainly have flourished, but hardly with the sturdy vigor it showed in Athens, where it became each man's way of liberty and law. From gutter to council chamber it proliferated, through the years of Athens' aggrandizement, blossoming at last in an imperial bureaucracy where nobody knew who he was, where the one-time allies of the city that conquered Persia cursed the shadow of the Ugly Athenian, while wistful liberals at home wondered what had become of the Athenian dream. It was in this world, and in this latter state of mind, that Aristophanes produced his first plays and won triumph, not for a political platform, but for the poetry which that world engendered, the drama of the city and the self.

City poetry, as we call it today, falls mainly into two categories: satire and the poetry of alienation. The poetry of alienation is personal, delicate, and subjective; satire is robust, socially oriented, and at least purportedly objective. A possible third class, poems in praise of certain cities, may be passed over. Such poems form a distinct genre, but they are distinguished, all of them from Rutilius Namatianus's "Farewell to Rome" to Carl Sandburg's "Chicago," by a certain distance from the object of their encomiums, a historical perspective, real or imagined, that sets them apart from the immediate involvement of city poetry proper. Cities can be praised from a distance; viewed closely, they prompt euphoria, revulsion, fear, and loss of identity, or else an attitude of mocking clinical observation—the detached, ironical stance of the social critic. The reaction is usually either one or the other. Aristophanes, however, managed both, thanks to his responsiveness and the protean medium of his various comic personae. It may not seem at once apparent that Aristophanes gives voice to any sense of alienation or loss of identity. Yet such alienation is in the very roots of the comedy that it was his business to produce. If he showed more interest in the cures for alienation than in the disease itself, that is because the mode of comedy, whatever its materials, is restorative—a positive creation out of the most negative matter, a rebirth, perhaps a ritual reenactment of the myth of spring's return, out of which comedy is supposed to have been born.

But the misty origins of comedy do not explain the originality of the comic poet. Aristophanes' plays—iridescent in wit and exuberance, earthy and airy at once, mixtures of pure realism and pure nonsense—have never seemed to me to deserve any of the charges of pamphleteering often directed at them by critics. Why could he not state his position on social improvement clearly and consistently, or, if responsibility were too much to ask of him, content himself with the satirist's joy in exposing crime and imposture and let his hearers draw some obvious moral? The moral was not obvious, so it has sometimes seemed best to give the poet the harmless motley of the clown. But something was still amiss with the clown; the cap was upside-down, or the bells seemed to toll instead of jingle. There was a lurking seriousness, even sorrow—but to look for it was like trying to identify a leading tone in the music of an aeolian harp.

For Aristophanes was as responsive as he was irresponsible, and every nerve end in his poetic body was continually awake and reacting to stimulus, twittering phrenetically in a kind of electronic response to the myriad mini-phenomena given off daily by that great radioactive mass, Athens. His pages are among the busiest in the history of poetry. His antennae pick up and transmit, in a rattling staccato, the lives of politicians, per-verts, panders, poets, pickle-sellers, oracle-sellers, decree-sellers, fortune-tellers, fortune-seekers, fortune-wasters, emis-saries, commissaries, cutpurses, cowards, harp-players, harbor-masters, harlots, tax-collectors, informers, Euripides, fakes, fools, foreigners, fishmongers, and philosophers—all the riffraff. To stage and satirize these types was the city-poet's task, and Aristophanes did it, as did his rivals Eupolis, Cratinus, and the others.

But there is always something more behind the noise, some-thing that is joined with, and yet different from, the steady

pageant of vice, fraud, and poisonous personalities. To call it a
streak of tenderness runs the risk of connoting a sentimental,
Dickensian mixture of laughter and tears, which won't do at all.
Aristophanes never suspends his irony. Nor can it be identified
with that more modern kind of sympathy, the twentieth-century
social critic's angry, activist response to squalor and misery.
This strain, this otherness one intuitively detects in Aristophanes, is something that runs deeper than social criticism; it
starts, and largely remains, in the secrecy of the individual soul.
The feeling we call alienation is probably the loneliest of all
feelings, universal, yet all but inexpressible; its true language is
silence, yet it is one of the principal fountains of poetry. It is
anything but a peculiarly modern feeling; it is probably inborn
from the moment of our being tossed into the world, though not
all people awaken to it. The remarkable thing is that we find it
in a poet of the Old Comedy, a medium that called for lam-
poon, parody, slapstick, and obscenity, for every form of
ridicule against the hoaxes and predators of the city, and even
for salubrious moralizing, but not for the voice of spiritual isolation in an alien world. That voice can be heard speaking with
poignancy in Sappho, more often with defiance in Archilochus;
it is heard from the tragic protagonists of Sophocles, and from
that most isolated of heroes, Achilles. But in Aristophanes it
comes as something over and above the call of comic conventions, and in its presence may lie the reason Aristophanes survived the ages, while Eupolis and Cratinus did not. Because of
it, his poetry has an edge even more fine than the edge of his
wit; or better, his wit owes much of its edge to the underlying
tremor of the individual heart at bay. Unlike the modern lyrist,
Aristophanes spends no time telling us directly about his own
alienation, though he might have used a parabasis (the section
of an Old Comedy in which the poet addresses the audience in
his own person) to admit such a confidence, as he does his
chagrin at the failure of the Clouds. His responses as a poet are

all transmitted through his characters, the people of his various, precarious worlds, jerry-built year after year for each festival of the drunken god.

The *Lysistrata* is almost wholly about alienation. It is a play in which we tend to think of the young women, for some reason; but the chorus is made up of old women, with much to say for themselves. Like the younger ones, they have joined in the struggle against the men to end the war and restore peace, their part being to seize the Acropolis while the younger women stage the notorious sex strike. Such action seems natural enough within the ensorcelled boundaries of an Aristophanic fantasy: to restore peace by an act of war, to restore sex by refusing it altogether is, of course, perfectly logical. But while it has been part of woman's role since the time of our grandmother Eve to sway man by her charm or, as in this case, the denial of them, the old women have been thrust into a position not quite so traditional. They have been turned into outright warriors, tough old harridans exchanging threats and blows with the chorus of old men and countering the attempt to burn them out of the Acropolis with generous buckets of cold water poured from the battlements. But then there comes a haunting touch. The old women recall their girlhood; they have no evident reason to do so, except that they are creatures of Aristophanes, born to enact his poetic will upon the stage. They say they will offer the tribute of good advice to the city, where they had been reared "splendidly, in all luxury" (640), performing the religious offices appointed for well-born girls at Athens:

As soon as I was seven, I served as bearer of the holy symbols,
Then at ten I ground the sacred meal for Athena;
Later, wearing a yellow robe, I danced the bear-dance at Brauron,
And when I was a fine young lady,
I carried a basket, with strung figs [i.e., in the procession at the
    Panathenaea].

[641–47]

The impact of these images of innocence and placid childhood, intruding suddenly on the raucous melee of the present, is incalculable. Once happy girls, these old women have been torn by time and war out of roles ordained, apparently, by city as by nature, and thrust into other, alien attitudes, to brazen them out as best they can. As bearers of men, they say, they too have a share in the city, but they do not say what it is; their words come pathetically like a plea for woman's very right to exist or have a role at all.

Yet there is no programmatic feminism here, or even, in all probability, much serious social reflection on the status of the Athenian woman. The stream of sympathy runs broader, and Aristophanes elicited sympathy for the male citizens as well. Old Philocleon in the *Wasps* suffers from a compulsive addiction to sitting jury duty. He is a man with a role, a stern judge, whose conscience has never in his life permitted him to vote for an acquittal; if by some mischance a defendant escapes, Philoclean goes to bed, sick. His sense of power is immense; he considers himself and his fellow jurors, though they work all day for three miserable obols, the most powerful men in the city. But alas, he is undeceived by his son who demonstrates, in a long debate, that he is merely the dupe of the big politicians, that his thruppence a day do not indicate control of the exchequer, and that he is, in fact, nothing. The old man's collapse is touching, adorned with tragic parody and the threat of suicide. Philocleon is changed, though not exactly reformed; we must beware of reading too simple a moral lesson. Judging is Philocleon's being, and the next we see of him he is at home conducting the trial of a dog indicted for stealing cheese. By an unconscionable trick, the dog is acquitted, and Philocleon collapses a second time. At the end of the play, he himself is a defendant on charges of drunkenness, assault, and multiple mayhem, a role not so likely to dissolve in thin air as his previous ones. But has he been brought around to reality? He seems more accurate to say that he has been brought around to unreality, from weighty judge to weightless chaff blown out of the grinding mill of the impersonal, faceless city. He has been changed not so much *from* what he was as *into* what he is.

It is always said of this play that it is a satire on the Athenian love of litigation. True but leaden, the observation takes no account of the sympathy that follows Philocleon from beginning to end, the same sympathy that follows Falstaff up Gad's Hill, or Buster Keaton towing an ocean liner with a rowboat. The power of the *Wasps* is not the blatantly obvious satire, any more than the point of the *Lysistrata* lies in a tendentious manifesto of women's rights. The power lies in the ironic transformation, in whose spell nothing, nobody, remains quite what it is but undergoes a change into an uneasy otherness—an elsehood, if one might have the word—and in the process becomes something not proper to itself or to anything, except to the wry world in which it is made to exist, and perhaps not perfectly to that. Transmogrification is intrinsic to the art of Aristophanes.

In the *Lysistrata*, one of the young women, unable to sustain the rigors of the sex strike, tries to return home by pretending that she is in the last stages of pregnancy. She shows her large belly to Lysistrata, claiming it's going to be a boy.

> *Lysis:* You weren't pregnant yesterday.
> *Girl:* Well, I am today.
>
> [745]

Lysistrata, feeling something hard and metallic, exposes the bulge for what it is, a helmet tucked under the girl's dress (740–52). In a play whose theme is war's battlement of the natural and sacred rites of fertility, what symbol could be more apposite than that the fruit of this young matron's womb should be not a male child, but a helmet? Nor is it any ordinary helmet, but Athena's own holy helm, lifted presumably from Phidias's great statue, the monstrous totem of imperial Athens herself. As this alien body is revealed in the place where, but for war's ruination of the ceremonies of love, a baby might have been, the girl's hoax grows heavy with symbolism. For all the hilarity, the jester's bells are muted, as they are also in the *Acharnians,* when the two starving little girls from Megara are transformed into pigs and sold by their starving father, to be fattened up for sacrificial victims (729ff.)—a scene that might pass for direct, serious protest of some kind, except that it turns out, by one of the ribald transfigurations of Greek slang,[1] that the two little urchins are destined to be offered only to Aphrodite, in a singularly ancient, persistent, and still popular form of ritual.

Certainly the transformations work the other way around, too, and may equally well mark the regeneration of the world or the self. The helmet is not the only symbol in the *Lysistrata* to be concealed under a garment. As the women begin to carry the day, the alien shafts of war are transformed in their turn and reappropriated by the triumphant cause. A herald arrives from Sparta, carrying what appears to be a spear under his cloak. He is promptly challenged by the Athenian magistrate, but all is well; the concealed spear is revealed to be no more than a prodigiously extended phallus, the harbinger of fertility's return. Spear and phallus, the prime dramatic polarities, are momentarily fused as the comic action, nearing its achievement of peace and domestic order, sweeps all before it. Mighty Sparta has been undone by a unilateral and nonnegotiable seizure of lust, and the herald has come to make peace. The Athenian magistrate is changed too. So antiquated at his first entrance that the women had dressed him in graveclothes and transformed him, so to speak, into a corpse, he has been favored by comedy's beneficent theme of rejuvenation and is now young enough to share the herald's problem and his readiness to capitulate. The beauty of comedy is that it can cure, for as long as its brief era lasts, the woes that set it in motion. The hero of the

1. [Whitman is referring to the Greek word χοιρίον, "piglet," slang for "vagina."]

Acharnians puts a shield to better use as a slop basin, while at the end of the *Peace*, helmets, now purposeless, become chamber pots, always useful, and spears gain a new future as props in a vineyard. All the alien objects are reincorporated, with magical ease, into a world restored by comic art.

But the alien self poses a still larger problem. Loss of role in society, or the discovery that one's role is contrary to one's conception of it, is isolating enough. But the farthest extreme of alienation is total loss of identity, which is the state of the ordinary man when the city has become too suffocating. Except in the *Frogs*, the central figure of every play of Aristophanes is an ordinary man or woman. But it is the *Acharnians*, perhaps, that dramatizes most poignantly this figure's imbecilic predicament in the metropolis. The play begins with a striking tableau of isolated individualism. There is supposed to be an assembly of the whole sovereign people of Athens; but as it happens, the whole sovereign people is late, presiding officers and all, and only one citizen is found on the Pnyx, a man whose name denotes his civic conscience—Dicaeopolis. He almost does not need to say anything; his solitary presence in the high assembly place is dramatic image enough, of an insignificance at once pathetic and grand. He has been waiting for hours, yawning, fidgeting, and counting up his sorrows and joys, the former numberless, the latter few—in fact, only four. He comes from the country but has been driven by the war, like everyone, to live inside the city walls. He is determined, if the machinery ever gets moving, to make a great outcry in favor of peace and against everything else. But he has yet to learn the full extent of his nonentity. When the assembly finally forgathers and business commences with the herald's cry, "Who wishes to speak?" a certain Amphitheus, who claims he is immortal and related to the gods, rises and says he has been commanded by them to make peace with Sparta, but needs travel expenses to get there. He is arrested immediately. Dicaeopolis tries to protest, but is ordered by the herald to shut up and sit down. Says Dicaeopolis:

By Apollo, I will not,
Unless the presidents preside for peace!
[59–60]

The herald ignores him and introduces ambassadors from the
great king. Dicaeopolis again protests and again is told to shut
up. The ambassadors are escorted in and proceed to explain
what they did with their munificent expense account on a mission to the great king eleven years before. Dicaeopolis can only
grumble and squirm, but is driven to renewed action when the
ambassadors introduce a minister from the Persian king, who is
really a well-known Athenian phony dressed up. Dicaeopolis
denounces him triumphantly, but the herald says for the third
time, "Shut up, and sit down!" Shortly, the assembly is ad-
journed, business concluded, but only after a gang of Thracian
mercenaries has robbed Dicaeopolis of a bunch of garlic he was
counting on for lunch. So much for the life of a citizen! Could
a man's identity be more decisively expunged? Could alienation
be more complete? Dicaeopolis does not think so. The garlic
perhaps had been too near a thrust. He will devise a cure, but
the disease is too deep-rooted for any known methods of political reform; it has struck far down into that irreducible unit of
existence, the unique, individual self, and threatened it with
annihilation. The cure must be radical, personal, *and* "de-
miurgic."

The concern with the identity, or alienation, of the self is a
private feeling that finds expression for the most part in the
personal lyric. When it appears in dramatic projection, it makes
for tragedy, and in the *Antigone* we have one example from the
Greeks of what might be called city tragedy. It is rarely found in
city comedy—Chaplin's *Modern Times* is exceptional—for the
idiom of city comedy is traditionally satiric, its concern social.
Aristophanes is able to combine the satiric voice of city comedy
with a more private, lyrical voice that I shall try to describe in
the last part of this chapter.

Aristophanes is often praised as a lyric poet, on the preposterous grounds that he occasionally introduces some graceful woodnotes about nightingales or elm trees in the spring. But his lyricism is neither so occasional nor so superficial; it underlies everything he wrote, deeply rooted in his poetic apprehension of the individual soul. This lyricism can make itself felt quite as well in a prayer to the muse to dump a big gob of spit on the head of a rival poet as it can in a twittering of elms. His satiric side has claimed more attention, but the tender, homeless strain of individual lyricism is ever present, qualifying and ultimately engulfing the satire in a vision that is less "keen and critical" than transcendent and redemptive.

Such a secret core, lurking within the multifarious interlocking conventions that make up the Old Comic scheme, gave to the art of Aristophanes at once an emotional range and poetic comprehensiveness not to be found elsewhere in the annals of city drama. The urbane masterpieces of Ben Jonson—*Volpone, The Alchemist, Bartholomew Fair*—though their satiric limits are expanded to embrace a surreal farcicality akin to the nonsense of Aristophanes, remain nonetheless satire. They were not excessively bitter, for Jonson's Juvenalian gifts of rhetorical hyperbole and morbid dissection of vice were balanced by a Horatian temperateness of outlook; yet these plays have little in their texture to recall the steady ground bass of compassion that resonates through Aristophanes' best works. It is heard as a constant reminder that the poet's work is positive, that he is building something, even as he lays waste the paltry, obnoxious, and constricting world of contemporary reality. This impalpable tone of compassion, this lyricism, is the music to which Aristophanes' comic edifices rise. Each one, grotesquely original and graceful in its grotesquerie, performs the function of a Prospero's isle in restoring true identity, "when no man was his own." *The Tempest* is a pastoral, and Aristophanes' works are city comedy; yet both encompass an imaginative reordering of the world through art, whether Prospero's, Peithetaerus's, or the dramatists' own; for little distinction can be made in a play where the protagonist is identifiable as the poet's sketch of spiritual power over what seems real.

In the apocalyptic perspective to which he sometimes attains, as well as in lyrical tone, Aristophanes indeed shows some affinity for the late Shakespearean romances. But such an achievement, in the realm of city comedy, could have been possible only for a Greek, and a Greek of the fifth century B.C. In this form, Ben Jonson once more, rather than Shakespeare, offers the natural foil for comparison, and contrast, of moral and dramaturgical structure. There is much in Jonson that is Aristophanic by way of wit, bawdry, grotesquerie, and joyous impudence. Both poets set up an antic and monstrous caricature of society; both react violently to the city's dismal perversion of the concepts of order and individual selfhood. But these two concepts, essential to the very idea of drama, were so divergently framed by the respective traditions of Aristophanes and Jonson that their final products, the plays themselves, seem at times almost totally different in genre. The aspiring individual of the Renaissance tended to carry the colors of Machiavelli against an order that, in the last analysis, could not be budged; the grander and dizzier his flight, the more certain was his fall. For the fifth-century Greek, or at least for Aristophanes, the frontiers of the cosmos, if not of the city, were not so rigid; the individual had more options, had he the wit to exercise them, and the temptations of the ultramundane were not foredoomed. Moral order was a thing to be created, while for the Elizabethan and Jacobean it was still a thing ordained.

The three plays of Jonson mentioned earlier share a common pattern, a structure of urban vice, complex in the extreme, built to a giddy pitch of involvement and risk, and finally exposed by some character who restores order, or at least some new equilibrium that may, in fact, be quite ironical. Actually, there is a kind of double exposure; the shrewd brains who direct the vicious intrigues—Volpone, Mosca, or Jeremy-Face—exploit a series of gulls, who are successively exposed as the embodiments of some vice, folly, or outright madness, before the central conspirators are themselves exposed. The character who does the exposing comes in various forms. Ultimately derived from the morality play, he is sometimes called a presenter, a kind of stage manager who unmasks, or "presents," the sins of the world in their true light for the edification of all. In satiric comedy, he blends easily into the poet's own assumed role of social critic, while in romantic drama he is the duke in disguise; Shakespeare's fools jump fitfully into and out of the part, delicately pinpointing the folly of others by analogy with their own. The presenter is a kind of supremely ironic God-figure, often wearing the mask of the vice, his original function being to bring justice about, with rewards for the good and punishment for the wicked.

This restoration of justice is a splendid moral goal, quite the sort of thing that satirists, from time immemorial, have been claiming as their high purpose and the justification for all their muckraking; and many critics, alas, believe them. But satire of the grand Roman tradition, from Juvenal to Jonson, is the product of a delight in indecent exposure; and the restoration of moral order at the end of *Volpone* is far from being its most satisfying part. To whose greater joy does Volpone at last fall? One is rather sorry to see him go. Jonson's genius is at its best when he creates these monsters of the underworld, from the cool, subtle Mosca to the hot, fat Ursula, the pig woman of *Bartholomew Fair*, contact with whom is like "falling into a whole shire of butter."

It was perhaps partly out of regard for these worthies, and partly because the world of James I was getting too grown up and sophisticated for morality drama, that Jonson, verging on the truly Aristophanic spirit, completely capsized the role of the presenter in *Bartholomew Fair* and in *The Alchemist*. In the former, he is a justice of the peace, disguised as a fool in order to expose the enormities of sin that flourish at the fair. But the disguise is truer than the office; Justice Overdo is gulled, robbed, beaten, and set in the stocks, while Enormity goes flourishing on in style. With the discovery of his own wife drunk, disorderly, and sick among the sinners, he can do no more to his intended victims than invite them home to dinner.

The Alchemist goes even further. There the arch-rogue Jeremy, alias "Face," turns his absent master's house into a buzzing center for inquity, where various greedy or lunatic dupes are brought in, dressed up, shaken down, and befuddled out of their wits and substance. Exposed and nearly trapped by a well-intentioned character, a would-be presenter, Face outpresents him and sends him flying. His triumph is ratified in the end, when the master returns and, far from setting things to rights, smiles like the god of comedy and accepts him with the words, "I will be ruled by thee in anything." In these two plays Jonson's wit—to which he himself paid unblushing deference—totally scuttled moral earnest, and we see how far city comedy has risen above the morality play. Jonson's satiric scheme gives a microcosmic picture of society engaged in a happy, Hobbesian game of dog-eat-dog up to the very end, when some killjoy appears and puts an end to the fun, or, alternatively and better, tries to but fails.

What would Aristophanes have thought of it all? We can be sure that he would have liked the justice in the stocks; he would have reveled in the language, the rumpus, the procession of swaggering, skulking, scheming practitioners of the devil's business; and he would have approved mightily when the conscienceless imagination of Face inverts the establishment and pockets the gold, with a "Heigh-ho, Helter-skelter, Uptails all, and a louse for the hangman." He would not, certainly, have been morally bothered. But he might have felt that two things were lacking, both fundamental to comedy as he envisioned it. He might have felt, for one thing, that the play would have been finer if the victory had been grander, had the world at large been affected, or somehow rewrought. In Jonson, nothing is tran-

scended or transformed. The world is not renewed. Thanks to
Face, old Master Lovewit gets a young wife and a stolen fortune
to spend on her; in a sense, his house will be renewing itself for
some time to come, and not to the tune of *Rock of Ages;* so
much is Dionysian. But Lovewit's house, though it stands for
the world, is only a microcosm. What renews the world is myth,
and that, in Jonson, is lacking.

The second thing that Aristophanes might have missed is a
full sized surrogate for man. There is no character in these city
comedies with whom we inevitably identify. Volpone is admir-
ably vigorous and resourceful, and Justice Overdo, in his way,
endearing, but most of us would prefer not to find ourselves in
them; neither are quite all human aspirations to be subsumed
under the winning attainments of Jeremy-Face. Sometimes one
of these characters, or the composite sum of them, may gain
universality by emerging as Natural Man—that ambiguous
specter of the Renaissance, later Blake's horror, today Freud's
cornerstone and everybody's problem. But no one in this popu-
lous gallery of human frailty represents the soul of man. Everyman, once necessary to the parent morality play, is nowhere to
be seen. As for the presenter, when there is one, his appeal is
akin to that of a policeman, which has limitations. By contrast,
Aristophanes' central comic figure was something of mightier
stature than such small schemers and moralists possess. He can
play the Presenter, among other things, but he is also a figure
framed to bear the weight of the greatest human aspirations and
to achieve them by transcendence and transformation, in a
grand, mythic renewal of the world. He is a lyrically felt figure,
who invites us to more than an acknowledgment of either his
native skill or moral soundness. He invites us to join our souls
with his, for he is the Myth of Ourself, and we have no choice
but to identify with him.

The plight of Dicaeopolis at the opening of the *Acharnians*
was sad indeed; call it alienation or whatever, it is the plight of
all the ordinary Athenians whom the Peloponnesian War and

its politicians had reduced to fribbles and plankton. By the time
the play's prologue is over, he is as nothing, save for the sole
spark of everlasting fire, which, as Plato says, Prometheus
planted in the hearts of men. Once the self has been cast out
upon itself, it has only its own devices. The cure is not social
reform, nor any complaisant self-adjustment that might bring
about repatriation. The cure must be re-creation of the
world—a thought that enters all our minds, a thought that once
entered the mind of God himself, when the perversities of men
became too much. No flood was at the command of Dicaeopolis, but Aristophanes' imagination was, and thanks to that,
the comic hero's loss of identity turns out to be not his end, but
his beginning. Having failed to bring his city around to making
peace, Dicaeopolis makes peace with Sparta by himself, and for
himself. This is his beginning as Promethean man.

The private peace could have been dramatized in any
number of ways; it could have been left a very small affair, for
instance, with just the hero and his family in their cottage
basking in peace, while the war clatters around them. That
would have been comical, but not enough. Dicaeopolis's peace,
though officially denied to all others, is like rising dough; it
spreads and engulfs the whole dramatic world, as figure after
figure from the ambience of war is assimilated, or annihilated,
by the sheer momentum of the protagonist's creative will. The
war becomes a flight of echoes in the background, a mere rumor
of war, while Dicaeopolis's open market fills the foreground of
the new world, fostering the happy trade of contraband with
what once were enemies, while the informers—presenters—
who try to stop it are beaten off with whips, or boxed up in
crates, like cracked pottery, and shipped out to Boeotia. For
climax, as the grand transformation nears completion, a new
pitiable figure appears: it is General Lamachus, the great warrior, who has fallen into a ditch and bumped his head, in the
effort to perpetuate the most absurd of all occupations. All is
reversed; by the time he is carried in, poor Lamachus seems to

be the only man in Greece who does not know the war is over. He is now the alien figure. Dicaeopolis's peace, though it was only for himself, has become the state of society.

How did this ordinary individual, so pathetically reduced at the beginning of the play, come by such capaciousness, such a colossal largeness that he bestrides the world and rides it into triumph? Whence could comedy, satirical city comedy at that, have derived so grand a human image, in which every man can find himself so much taller than he dreamed? Not from Dionysian ritual, that is certain. Comedy got it, or at least Aristophanes got it, from tragedy. Even as the grave and edifying specter of the morality play stood behind Jacobean city comedy, so too the spirit of tragedy, grand and heroic, stood behind Old Comedy, or better stood beside it, for comedy was not much the younger of the two. Tragedy was by all odds the predominating poetic form of the fifth century; many have observed that Old Comedy could not live without tragedy, meaning, live without it as a source for parody. But tragedy's contribution consisted of more than that. The Jacobean satirists inherited from the moralities the moral purpose, or the claim to it, which has always accompanied literary satire. Tragedy's moralizing was not so downright as that of morality drama; it groped and explored among the great issues. What it had to give was not a preestablished moral order presided over by God, but a figure in quest of order, a creative, passionate selfhood, active yet suffering, alone and great upon the world's spiritual frontiers, namely, the tragic hero.

At first, surely, comedy found immediate access to this figure through the obvious door of parody. But so central, so much the *personnage régnant* of fifth-century Athenian life and thought was the image of the isolated hero, man against the sky, that comedy was bound to make greater use of him than for parody alone. As a native of Athenian soil, he could be as proper to comedy as to tragedy, and Aristophanes made him so.

At this point the argument may seem to be getting perverse.

What can city alienation have to do with heroic isolation? Juxtaposed, the terms jangle cacophonously, evoking opposite literary worlds. But the world of Old Comedy is nothing if not jumbled and perverse, and the *Acharnians* alone is sufficient to reveal how this dissonant conjunction was contrived to begin with and then resolved into harmony. It almost seems as if Aristophanes were deliberately revealing his own comic method. Dicaeopolis has made peace, but is challenged by the chorus of charcoal burners from Acharnae; they want revenge for their ruined vineyards and will have no thought of peace. Dicaeopolis persuades them to listen, and prepares to give an address explaining his position. But first he must put on the persona of a persuasive, nay tragic, speaker, some master of cunning rhetoric, a commodity found in abundance in the possession of Euripides. Fortunately, the tragedian's house is handy, like everything on the comic stage, and Dicaeopolis goes to borrow the tragic costume, that is, rags, and the compelling rhetoric, of Euripides' bedraggled hero Telephus, whose story he had staged thirteen years before. Euripides obliges, and Dicaeopolis, equipped with various props and accoutrements in addition to the all-necessary rags, steps into the role of Telephus, the wounded king in beggar's guise, who pleaded his desperate cause, at risk of life, before the Atreidae. In this new role, Dicaeopolis proceeds to make his speech on behalf of peace, staking his head on the result. It is a fine speech, all about the causes of the Peloponnesian War, and scholars have ransacked it for gobbets of historical truth. The point, however, is not what Dicaeopolis says, but what he has become; he has become the tragic hero Telephus, and even calls himself by that name.

Something more than parody is involved here. For a space of 300 lines, Aristophanes' play turns into a montage upon the *Telephus* of Euripides, a sort of double exposure that creates a frantic transformation, something Aristophanic through and through. Two figures representing city alienation and heroic isolation have been welded into a single, anomalous shape em-

bodying a kind of truth not to be found in the rhetorical acroba-
tics that his tongue performs. Still the ordinary citizen, yet also
the king in disguise, Dicaeopolis has literally become two things
at once, as any man of practical theater, envisioning the production, will understand. Such a feat falls properly within the realm
of sorcery, but for the benefit of those who like mathematical
proof, it may be put as an equation:

$$\text{Heroic Isolation} \times \text{City Alienation} = \frac{1}{\text{Everbody}}$$

for everybody is won over, and that's the mathematics of it.

At least, almost everybody is won over. Lamachus is not. As
climax to Dicaeopolis's victory Lamachus, Raw Head and
Bloody Bones, springs threateningly onto the stage in full armor, to be systematically dismantled by the hero's intrepid wit
and driven to retreat, his shield transformed into a slop-pail and
his crest into a feather to assist emesis. Jostled by all the
slapstick, the dramatic center of this scene can easily be passed
over in reading, but it cannot but stand out unmistakably in a
stage production. Dicaeopolis jeers at Lamachus with a triple-
forte obscenity; Lamachus retorts:

Lam: Do you dare to talk like that to me, a general—you beggar!
Dic: What? Me, a beggar?
Lam: Well, who are you?

[593ff.]

Put so directly, the identity question can be answered only in
terms of what the dramatic action has so far achieved. Dropping
his disguise, Dicaeopolis says simply, "A good citizen" (595);
but as the rags fall away, a new man stands forth, neither Telephus the beggar-king nor the Dicaeopolis who was nothing.
These roles have been knitted together to form a new, real self, a
good citizen of royal stature, a Promethean self heroically alone

against a hostile world just beginning to measure his mighty dimensions.

The tragic guise has worked. Like the presenter, Dicaeopolis unmasks himself to unmask the Bugbear of War, denouncing him for an impostor. His words are satire, but their meaning is the song of rebirth. He does not exactly restore law and order, as the presenter would; he restores what seemed lost in the prologue, his identity as man, the myth of ourself. Whatever order he establishes thereafter will be the order of himself, as is presently demonstrated in the scenes that follow in the new redeemed world of Dicaeopolis's open market.

It has been repeatedly, and truly, said that the Aristophanic hero pursues a quest. A quest is a heroic enterprise, but the most heroic quest of all is the quest of the true self. Heroic literature, from the *Iliad* on, is about little else. Dicaeopolis's great effort has often been called a quest for peace, but in fact, the peace, in the form of a thirty-year-old wineskin, is achieved with relative ease early in the play. The struggle that is dramatized, via the disguise as Telephus, is a heroic quest for identity before the universe, an identity lost or obscured in the cheapening world. In the *Iliad*, when Agamemnon insulted and made light of Achilles, he diminished his selfhood; instead of responding with the sword, Achilles shifted levels and referred the question of his value to Zeus. In response to the herald's demolishing "Sit down and shut up," Dicaeopolis shifts levels, refers the matter to tragedy, and seeks his selfhood in the guise of beggary and kinship, a paradigm that turns out to be both decorous and efficacious.

The differences between the tragic and comic modes should not be allowed to obscure large structural resemblances, or the fact that parody, which could never reduce tragedy, could and did enlarge comedy. The rewards, of course, differ. In reparation for his tainted honor and the stolen Briseis, Achilles receives honor from Zeus, heightened spiritual knowledge, and early death. In recompense for his shattered selfhood—and stolen garlic—Dicaeopolis receives two little Megarian pig-girls, Copaic eels, countless items of poultry, the prize in a drinking-match, two strapping harlots, and an invitation to dinner with the high priest of Dionysus. *Suum cuique.* The difference in the ending of the rituals, the one in tragic stillness, the other in a revel, simply points, as Aristophanes would maintain, to the infinite superiority of comedy, whose quests are accomplished among vistas the limited vehicle of tragedy never attains.

As an example of the poetry of the city, it is hard to see how the *Acharnians* could be surpassed. There is plenty of direct satire: the hawkish informer, the militarist, the war-profiteer, the phony ambassadors, the snake-oil orator—satire's impaling lance holds up their wriggling forms, one and all. But the power lies in Aristophanes' lyrical responsiveness to the human soul in the midst of it all—confused, betrayed, lost, isolated, and heroic; slowly attaining, through marvels of dramaturgy, the mythic shape of humanity as individual. And what is meant by myth? Myth germinates in societies, reflecting their outlook and aspirations. Its terms are either cosmic, in which case myth represents the life and structure of the world, or individual, in which case myth recounts the life of the hero. The fantasy that Aristophanes constructs in his greatest plays is founded on the second of these, though the first, the life of the world, inevitably swings into view. It is into this great mythic paradigm that Dicaeopolis merges, as does Peithetaerus in the *Birds*, and even, though less completely, Philocleon and Lysistrata. On the satiric level, Dicaeopolis is the presenter—Greek style— exposing crime and imposture; but simultaneously, he is the heroic individual self, achieving a suprasocial victory in the context of no less than the world as a whole. Jonson could turn a house in London, or a fairgrounds, into a microcosm of the world, but he never quite put into it the individual who could be Everyman; Aristophanes could find his way, via tragedy and the poetry of alienation, to the myth of the hero, the Greek

Everyman. Myth is greater than microcosm, even as the hero, the seeker and builder of order, is truer and dramatically more viable than the preestablished order of God and the Christian Presenter. In Aristophanes the two voices of city poetry meet, satire and lonely lyric, corresponding to the two basic polarities of fictional character, the social stereotype and the character who represents man with his inner life. Tragedy could hardly exist without the second, or comedy without the first, but Aristophanes stages both and speaks for both, having devised a poetic language such as few poets have ever wielded—tender, derisive, plaintive, raucous, grand—a language that enables him to rejoice as much as any satirist in the horrors he exposes, without leaving the least touch of prurience in the air. There is no moralizing. Each time the hero annihilates an impostor, the creature does not grovel in humiliation or promise to reform; he explodes into nothingness, and his destroyer adds a cubit to his own stature. Aristophanes offers no code or creed; he reforges the self, and the world in its wake.

The *Acharnians* is not to be taken as a general pattern for all the plays, but it offers a certain vantage point for viewing the others. Some are quite different. Even the *Peace*, which is often treated as a hasty, even weak, reworking of the *Acharnians*, actually is wholly different, despite the common theme of peace and the superficial resemblance between Trygaeus and Dicaeopolis. The *Peace* is not a city play at all, nor does it ever raise the problem of the individual. The goddess Peace is alienated—she's buried alive—but the hero Trygaeus has no trouble with his identity; he states it early in the play, and his name—Wine-Lees—associates him as strictly with the country as Dicaeopolis's name links him to the city. His lack of any great struggle has caused the *Peace* to be criticized for lack of plot and conflict. The play is a country frolic, a pastorale whose lyricism is now communal and hymnal, rather than personal.

In the earlier plays the heroic potential is less fully deployed; Philocleon's loss of role leads to no great world transformation and triumph, though he does enact the transubstantiation of a flute-girl and a torch; but his boundless resilience assures us that in him the spark of selfhood survives and will survive, however delimited by his realistic son and the ever-present judiciary.

The *Clouds* is set a little apart by its special topic, not to mention its two versions. It can be seen as an attempt to reorient a baffled, outmoded self toward the world of the new education that only baffles it the more for trying. It is city poetry, insofar as the bucolic Strepsiades is swindled by the urbane Socrates, but the satire is narrowly focused on the intellectuals of the day, and the hero neither transcends anything, comprehends anything, nor invites identification.

The *Knights* is almost pure satire, from beginning to end, albeit satire of baroque breadth and extravagance, an enormous charade presenting the varieties of political corruption. The identity problem is not dramatized for any individual character, for the Sausage-Seller, once advised of his destiny, proceeds without hesitation or doubt, and Demos, whose true self is restored, is not an individual but a corporate body, the Sovereign State. As for the Paphlagonian, he can parody a tragic hero at the moment of his fall, but not step into the role; he provides a good exemplar for the difference between ordinary paratragic effect and the kind of functional dramatic montage found in the merger of Dicaeopolis and Telephus.

It was really not until the *Birds*, in 414, that Aristophanes again produced city poetry that used both the satiric and the mythic voice. Peithetaerus is so alienated by the city that he has turned his back on it altogether in an effort to return to nature, as to some happy womb where no problems exist. At first, no doubt, it seems as if he were rather the opposite of Dicaeopolis, no fighter, but an inconsequential escapist looking for Utopia, or at least some alternative society. Yet through the opening scenes, one hears the voice of despair and isolation amid the loss of all that the city seemed to promise. Athens is a free city—free for all to be taxed and fined; a lyric voice cries, Give up the cooked for the raw, and live with the birds, who are really free. The idyllic sweetness of bird life grows steadily more pressing for 200 lines, culminating in the Hoopoe's Aubade to the Nightingale and the summoning of the Birds to foregather. But as soon as they enter, Peithetaerus comes to himself. Late, but decisively, he realizes his destiny as man: to put on aspiring wings and grasping talons, to become a god by joining the animal world, and to put down the Olympians—those archimpostors who have so mismanaged everything. The heroic soul cannot aim much higher. It is the myth of the hero again, the individual limned against the universe, now fired by a presumptuousness that can lead only—to success.

The birds, too, realize their destiny. They give up the raw for the cooked, build a city, and at once become really dangerous. The world's great age begins anew, the primeval theomachies return. Moreover, the New City, like all cities, immediately begins to collect vermin. The series of satirical vignettes that follows offers the fullest presentation in all Aristophanes of the stock types that must be set up, derided, knocked down, and dispersed, so that the self may reign supreme. And if this same self, this Peithetaerus, is not only the supreme presenter but also the supreme pretender, the heroic impostor, that fact may arise from his maker's new perspective on cities and on man, individual and collective alike.

The *Birds* is a delicate play, yet grand; whimsical, yet deeply sardonic. Peithetaerus's victory is more complete even than Dicaeopolis's; but where the *Acharnians* ends in joy, the *Birds* ends in delirium, as if the myth of human selfhood, having passed all human bounds and entered the realm of the immortals, has outstripped the meaning of humanity, and therewith all meaning. The *Acharnians* tells the myth of the hero as it comes in folktales, following the pattern so well defined by anthropology and comparative folklore. The hero is born and raised in obscurity, like Dicaeopolis at the beginning; he comes upon a token or talisman that gives him access to superhuman power—the thirty-year-old wineskin of peace; he appears and states his claim—Telephus; he overcomes a monster— Lamachus; he wins the princess—the two strumpets; and he reigns happily ever after.

The *Birds* has all this too, but it reaches even higher; the Myth of Ourself moves onto the cosmic level. At the very moment of his realizing his heroic potential, as Peithetaerus resolves to depose the gods, the Myth of the Hero, the individual life of man, is joined to the worldwide Myth of the Succession in Heaven; Peithetaerus becomes king of the gods, and his princess is not an agreeable human strumpet, but Lady Sovereignty, very like Athena herself. The myth is glorious, the decorum of its enactment flawless, the poetic rhetoric sustaining and compelling throughout. In the *Birds* myth and irony have combined to make a city drama that suggests, in its airy transparency, the unreality of all cities, and therewith of the humanity that makes them. One could not go further, either with satire or with the lyric of the frontier itself.

At least, Aristophanes did not. The *Birds* is the last of the real city plays. In the *Lysistrata* three years later, the strain of alienation is almost continuous, and the heroic self is hinted at in the firm, though eventually self-effacing Lysistrata. But satire is almost totally lacking, and the charming choruses that end the play belong properly to the myth of the Golden Age, a country myth later to be found congenial to the pastoralists, poets so dazed and excluded by what the city had become by then that it could no longer be their theme.

It could be objected that terms such as "alienation" and "city poetry" do not belong among the Greeks. All Greek poetry after Homer and Hesiod might in a sense be called city poetry, but for us to call it so suggests the preoccupations of modernity and the work of Cavafy or William Carlos Williams. As for alienation, it is a twentieth-century, or at earliest nineteenth-century disease generated by the Industrial Revolution. The terms may indeed be indecorous; they come close, perhaps, to jargon. But the objection, to be just, ought to be followed by a list of better terms meaning the same things. There is no Greek equivalent for our "alienation," though Democritus's ἀμηχανίη (frag. B 285 DK) or Dicaeopolis's verb ἀπορῶ (Acharnians 31) suggest it. Anyway, it is not a matter of terms, but of feeling; was Aristophanes capable of feeling what we call alienation, so that in our jargon we might, however, inelegantly, refer to it as such? We cannot ask him, but we can ask Plato, who knew him.

In the *Symposium*, Plato puts into the mouth of the tipsy poet a speech about love, in accordance with the agreed procedure for the party (189c–193d). The speech has occasioned much speculation about its origin: Was this something that Aristophanes actually said or something that Plato made up? There is nothing exactly like it in Aristophanes' extant works, but neither does it sound much like Plato's usual kind of imagination. The sane assumption is that Plato knew his man, and that he, the dramatically gifted inventor of the dialogue, in which he recreated the personality of Socrates and others, gave Aristophanes the kind of speech he would be likely to make. At the very least, it strikes us as convincingly Aristophanic. It is a comic myth that tells how men were originally twice what men are now; they had four arms, four legs, a double body with sexual members facing both ways, and a head with two Janus-like faces. They were formidable, so much so that they threatened, as in the succession myth of Hesiod's *Theogony*, to depose the gods. In alarm, Zeus split each of them in two with lightning so that they became the relatively harmless bipeds we are today. But since that time, the several bipeds wander the earth, each looking for his other half, and never content even when he is lucky enough to find it. For although these lovers, once reunited, spend their whole lives together, in uninterrupted contemplation of each other, "Yet," says the speaker, "they cannot explain what they desire. For the intense yearning each of them has toward the other does not appear to be the desire for sexual intercourse, but for something else that the soul of either evidently yearns for and cannot express, and of which it has only an obscure and doubtful presentiment. . . . And the reason is that human nature was originally one and we were a whole, and the desire and pursuit of that whole is called love."

Behind all the grotesquerie, there is something in Aristophanes' speech in the *Symposium* that brings to mind Shelley's *Alastor* and the High Romantic quest for the soul within the soul. One may question whether that quest was dependent on the Industrial Revolution or any historical event—even on the city, for that matter. It seems to be as ancient as the psyche itself. Aristophanes' speech has no title, but if it had to be given one, he or Plato might, in default of ancient terminology, be willing to call it "The Myth of Alienation."

Bibliography of
Cedric H. Whitman

BOOKS

Orpheus and the Moon Craters (poems). Middlebury, Vt.: Middlebury Press, 1941.

Sophocles: A Study of Heroic Humanism. Cambridge, Mass.: Harvard University Press, 1951. Award of Merit, American Philological Association.

Homer and the Heroic Tradition. Harvard University Press, 1958. Christian Gauss Prize, United Chapters of Phi Beta Kappa.

Aristophanes and the Comic Hero. Martin Classical Lectures Series, no. 19. Harvard University Press, 1964.

Abelard (narrative poem). Harvard University Press, 1965.

Euripides and the Full Circle of Myth. Loeb Classical Monographs Series. Harvard University Press, 1974.

Musaeus, *Hero and Leander* (translation). Loeb Classical Library. Harvard University Press, 1975.

Fifteen Odes of Horace (translation). Lunenburg, Vt.: Stinehour Press, 1980.

Chocorua and Other Poems. Dublin, N.H.: Wm. L. Bauhan, 1982.

ARTICLES

"The Vitality of the Greek Language and Its Importance Today." Lecture delivered at the Greek Orthodox Cathedral Evangelismos,

Boston, Mass., November 20, 1953. Office of Greek Education Bureau, New York, 1954, 11 pp.

"Two Passages in the *Ion* of Euripides." *Classical Philology* 59 (1964):257–259.

"Aristophanes." In *Collier's Encyclopedia* 2 (1965), pp. 603–607.

"Apocalypse: *Oedipus at Colonus*." In *Sophocles, A Collection of Critical Essays*, edited by Thomas Woodard. Englewood Cliffs, N.J.: Prentice-Hall, 1966, pp. 146–74 (reprinted from *Sophocles: A Study of Heroic Humanism*).

"Das Rätsel Sophokles: Die Klassizistische Sehweise." In *Sophokles*, edited by Hans Diller. Wege der Forschung, vol. 95. Darmstadt, 1967, pp. 11–35 (translation from *Sophocles: A Study of Heroic Humanism*, ch. 1).

"Greece: Classical Period." In *Encyclopaedia of World Drama*. New York: T. Y. Crowell, 1969, pp. 372–92.

"Ληκύθιον ἀπώλεσεν." *Harvard Studies in Classical Philology* 73 (1969):109–112.

"Why Not the Classics? An Old-Fashioned View." *Daedalus* (special issue, *The Future of the Humanities*) 98 (1969):809–14.

"Hera's Anvils." *Harvard Studies in Classical Philology* 74 (1970):37–42.

"Existentialism and the Classic Hero." In *Das Alterum und jedes neue Gute: Festschrift für Wolfgang Schadewaldt zum 15. März, 1970*. Stuttgart: Kohlhammer, 1970, pp. 99–115.

"Sophocles: *Ajax* 815–824." *Harvard Studies in Classical Philology* 78 (1974):67–69.

"Sequence and Simultaneity in *Iliad* N, Ξ, O." *Harvard Studies in Classical Philology* 85 (1981): 1–15 (with Ruth Scodel).

REVIEWS

R. Aubreton, *Démétrius Triclinius et les recensions médiévales de Sophocle*. *American Journal of Philology* 73 (1952): 325–28.

C. Kerényi, *The Gods of the Greeks*. *Journal of American Folklore* 66 (1953):89–91.

H. Schrade, *Götter und Menschen Homers*. *Erasmus* 7 (1954):553–57.

R. M. Dawkins, *More Greek Folktales*. *Journal of American Folklore* 69 (1956):76–77.

B. M. W. Knox, *Oedipus at Thebes*. *American Journal of Philology* 80 (1959):76–80.

G. M. Kirkwood, *A Study of Sophoclean Drama*, and H. D. F. Kitto, *Sophocles: Dramatist and Philosopher*. *The Phoenix* 14 (1960):175–77.

R. Payne, *The Gold of Troy: The Story of Heinrich Schliemann and the Buried Cities of Ancient Greece*. *The Classical World* 53 (1960):259–60.

David Barrett, ed. and trans., *Aristophanes: The Frogs and Other Plays*. *Arion* 7 (1968):422–26.

MISCELLANEOUS

Ode. Two readings for Joshua Whatmough on his retirement from Harvard University, May 29, 1963.

Memorial Minute for Thomas J. Wilson, Harvard University, May 5, 1970.

Foreword to *Eighteen Texts: Writings by Contemporary Greek Authors*, edited by Willis Barnstone. Harvard University Press, 1972.

Foreword to *Comparative Studies in Greek and Indic Meter*, by Gregory Nagy. Harvard University Press, 1974.

"Daphnis Retires" (poem) on the occasion of John H. Finley, Jr.'s retirement as Eliot Professor of Greek Literature, *Harvard Magazine* 78 (June 1976): 53–55.

Foreword to *Homage to the Tragic Muse*, by Angelos Terzakis. Boston: Houghton Mifflin, 1978.

Poems published in *New Republic*, *Poetry*, *Arion's Dolphin*, *padan aram*, *The Anthology of Magazine Verse and Yearbook of American Poetry* (1980), and elsewhere.

Vita of Cedric H. Whitman

Born December 1, 1916, Providence, Rhode Island

Robert Frost Fellow, Breadloaf School of English (summer, 1941)
Harvard College, A.B. *summa cum laude*, Phi Beta Kappa (1943)
Harvard University, Ph.D. (1947)

Instructor in Classics, Harvard, 1947–1950
Assistant Professor, Harvard, 1950–1954
Associate Professor, Harvard, 1954–1959
Professor, Harvard, 1959–1966
F.R. Jones Professor of Classical Greek Literature, Harvard, 1966–1974
Eliot Professor of Greek Literature, Harvard, 1974–1979

Chairman, Department of the Classics, 1960–1966
Editor, *Harvard Studies in Classical Philology*, 1957–1964
Advisory Editor, *Clio*, 1970–1979
Member, Board of Directors, College Year in Athens
Member, American Philological Association, Archaeological Institute of
America, Modern Greek Studies Association

Award of Merit, American Philological Association, 1952, for *Sophocles:
A Study of Heroic Humanism*
Christian Gauss Prize, United Chapters of Phi Beta Kappa, 1958, for
Homer and the Heroic Tradition
American Academy of Arts and Sciences, 1960–1979
Guggenheim Fellow, 1961–62, 1976–1977
National Endowment for the Humanities Grant for collecting Modern
Greek Shadow Theatre on tapes, film, and slides, 1969 (summer)
American Philosophical Society grant for continuation of Greek Shadow
Theatre project, 1970 (summer)
Academy of Literary Studies, 1974–1979

Died June 5, 1979, Cambridge, Massachusetts
Buried in Middletown, Rhode Island
A *Service of Thanksgiving for the Life of Cedric Hubbell Whitman*,
Harvard University, The Memorial Church, October 25, 1979.
Remarks by John H. Finley, Emily D.T. Vermeule, Robert S.
Fitzgerald. 14 pp.

Index

Library of Congress Cataloging in Publication Data

WHITMAN, CEDRIC HUBBELL.
The heroic paradox

"Bibliography of Cedric H. Whitman": p.
Includes index.
1. Greek literature—History and criticism—Addresses,
essays, lectures. I. Segal, Charles, 1936–
II. Title.
PA3061.W47   880'.9'001   82-5155
ISBN 0-8014-1453-9   AACR2

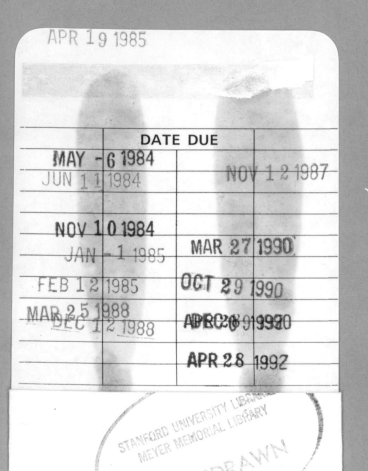